THE WEALTH OF

A SPIRITUAL WOMAN

Reverend Linda "SHAHEERAH" Beatty

TO SOW THE FALLOW SOIL

James C. Winston
Publishing Company, Inc.
Trade Division of Winston-Derek Publishers Group, Inc.

First printing

The author of this book does not dispense medical advice nor prescribe the use of any technique as a form of treatment for physical or mental problems without the advice of a physician either directly or indirectly. In the event you use any of the information in this book neither the author nor the publisher can assume any responsibility for your actions. The intent of the author is only to offer information of a general nature to help you in your quest for personal growth.

PUBLISHED BY JAMES C. WINSTON PUBLISHING COMPANY, INC.
Nashville, Tennessee 37205

Library of Congress Catalog Card No: 94-60969
ISBN: 1-55523-721-5

Printed in the United States of America

This book is dedicated to my "everything" God.
To my two grandmothers who are in spirit realm,
Lillie and Pernell.
To my mother, Rebeccca, and my father, Carl.

To my gifted daughter, Brandyn, and my
extraordinary son, Paptu.
To Bobbie for your loving support.
To Iyanla Vanzant for her love and encouragement.

To Callie Hoover, my first truth teacher.
To Jack Boland, Johnnie Coleman and Martha Jean,
"The Queen," the three dynamos whose ministries
catapulted my life. To my minister, friend and sister,
Rev. Argentina Glasgow, and my church home,
Detroit Unity Temple, whose love keeps me in flight.

To all of my sisters and brothers,
those who are awake
and those who are still sleep.

႗᪐

TABLE OF CONTENTS

Preface

Since 1974 I have been counseling with women and facilitating workshops from coast to coast. As a result of my work I have categorized the issues that women are most concerned about into four areas: **mothering, men, health** and **money**. This book is my offering to women because women are still so mentally oppressed and repressed in the world and God wants to set them free.

Women are important to God. I once heard a tape by Bishop T. Jakes, and his message really set me on fire. He said, "Women are the doors of life. If it gets here on this plane, it has to come through a woman." Everything we have, desire, or want comes from Mother Earth. Everything is made of dirt — money, house, bodies, our food, buildings and cars. Mother Earth supplies everything and just like the woman, she's not revered. There is a shameful imbalance in the world and now is the time for us to make a difference.

We don't need to become a man or to become like the worst of men. I see so many women in corporate America now who dress like men and try to act like men. What we need is to understand who we are in God and allow God to do the awesome exploits he desires to do in our lives.

Inside of a woman's body was placed a womb. God hovered upon the womb of Mary and she birthed the "word". Yet too many churches still say women shouldn't be allowed to be in a pulpit and speak the word. I beg to differ! She birthed the word, she can certainly speak it! God is pouring his spirit out upon all flesh. Open your heart and your mind with a prayerful spirit and drink, my sister, from this fountain. Drink this living water that will quench your thirst for "life and living" forever.

Chapter I

WHAT IS A SPIRITUAL WOMAN?

'Those who are led by the Spirit of God are sons and daughters of God.'   (Romans 8:14)

Before we can become wealthy spiritual women we must first understand what Spirit is. In John 4: 24 it states that 'God is Spirit.' Spirit is God, the "moving" force in the universe. Spirit is the "breath" of God. Your breath is Spirit breathing through you.

Our spiritual selves have nothing to do with religious affiliations. Through religious affiliations we may have learned about this part of ourselves; however, the relationship must be developed within an individual's heart. It is a very intimate relationship. It is a relationship that we sometimes find difficult to write about and speak about because words have an end and spirit doesn't. It's infinite. God cannot be contained in a religion or a book because God is too vast and awesome to fit into our limited concepts.

In John 3:5,6 we find, 'Verily, verily I say unto thee except a woman be born of water *and* of the Spirit, she can not enter into the kingdom of God. That which is born of flesh is flesh and that which is born of Spirit **is Spirit.**'

The Spirit is already a part of you.
You must become CONSCIOUSLY aware of it.

'Behold, I stand at the door and knock, if any woman hears my voice and opens the door, I will come to her, sup with her and she with me.' (Rev. 3:20)

When we receive Christ into our hearts, we become children of God. In Bell Hooks' book, *Sisters of the Yam*, she says, *"Living a life in the spirit, a life where our habits of being enable us to hear our inner voices, to comprehend reality with both our hearts and our minds, puts us in touch with divine essence."* Until we have that one-on-one experience, we will constantly be longing and dissatisfied. Nothing and no one can fill this longing but Spirit.

We are **"spiritual"** beings having a **"physical"** experience. Realize that you are living in two worlds. **The invisible world is the "real" one.** Why? Because that's were everything comes from. **The visible world is the effect. The invisible world is the cause.**

Woman is made up of Spirit, Soul and Body. Spirit is the unchanging and eternal part of us. God is Spirit; Soul is the clothing of the Spirit; Body is the external clothing of the Soul.

Spirit takes the deep things of God and reveals Truth to woman. In John 16:13 it says, 'When the Spirit of Truth comes he will guide you into **all** truth.' The Spirit will show you things to come. The Spirit won't allow you to be ignorant, but will reveal hidden mysteries unto you. *Spirit won't let nothing slip up on you and nobody.*

You are an idea in the mind of God. Read Genesis 1:27: 'God created man in his own image, in the image of God he created him; **male and female,** He created them.' ("Man" means male and female.)

We have both feminine and masculine faculties. When we think, use logic and our rational minds, we are utilizing our masculine faculty. When we are into our feelings and our intuition we are utilizing our feminine faculty. When I am out in the marketplace negotiating and planning, I am using my masculine faculties When I come home, I know how to be a woman and be more into my feminine self.

Suffering results for every woman who believes that she is in bondage to the flesh and to the things of the flesh. Suffering results because that belief is a limited belief and you are so much more than a body. We must "arise" and go to Mother/Father God. Rise out of the darkness of ignorance and realize that we are Spirit, Soul, and Body.

We are spiritual beings living in a spiritual universe and governed by "spiritual" laws. We don't have to feel we are controlled by outside appearances. We can see things as they truly are — **"appearances."** They have come in order that they may pass, that's right, pass right on out of our lives. When seeming challenges come, we can become still and know the truth that we are Daughters of the Creator. We are children of the mighty, living God who wills that we experience "absolute good." Regardless as to what others think, say or do, we can hold on to "truth" and the truth will manifest accordingly.

We suffer every time we forget who we really are and **whose** we really are. The pain is a **signal** to motivate us to "arise" and to go to a high mountain, a higher place in consciousness where we can experience the love and peace of God and see things from a higher viewpoint.

Spiritual women must rise often to the truth that we are 'heirs' (Romans 8:17) — heirs to all wisdom, love, life, substance, and power. We have it all. We no longer have to suffer because of death. Jesus overcame the grave! He resurrected to demonstrate that the grave couldn't hold him and that death couldn't destroy the temple not made by hands.

We believe that Spirit is indestructible and eternal. We understand that our physical bodies are mortal. Yet we are in touch with that immortal part of ourselves. I heard Rev. Cecilia Bryant, author of *Kiamsia*, speak at a women's conference in New York and she said (I paraphrase somewhat), "With the possession of the knowledge that one day we will die physically, our time becomes important to us. We realize that **our time is our life** and that it becomes increasingly important what we do with our time. We become less and less willing to allow others to prioritize our time for what they think is important for us to do."

It's important to carve out time for yourself. Taking time in the silence was something that Jesus did a lot. He went away in the mountain, alone. As you practice stilling your mind, sitting and just listening, you'll be surprised at the things that will come to you. In this stillness you can regain a sense of the Creator and Its love. Everyone needs quiet time and taking this time, sisters, is not a luxury, *it's essential*. Carve out the time for yourself. Get your appointment book and write in some time for this activity.

Sisters tell me all the time, "I don't have time, I'm too busy." "You *must* find the time," I tell them. When you find the time to be in the Presence of God, then you will have more time added unto you. Spending time with God will cause you to be more productive and it will make your work and days smoother, more peaceful and supernaturally prosperous.

As you practice the silence, you will notice that you are stronger mentally, emotionally and physically. **As you practice the silence, whatever needs to be healed is healed.** When you enter into your outer life, you will have more to give to others, for you have filled up your cup and you have plenty to give.

Chapter II

SEEK YE FIRST THE KINGDOM OF GOD

'To her who dwelleth in the secret place of the Most High there is promised immunity from the deadly pestilence, the snare, terror by night.' (Psalms 91)

What is the Kingdom of God? *Lessons In Truth* by Emilie Cady says "it is a **secret** place because it is a place of meeting between the Christ at the center of your being and your consciousness — a hidden place into which no outside person can either induct you or enter himself. So our elder brother, Jesus, tried to convey to us through so many parables that it was not a place outside of ourselves, as he said, 'The kingdom of God is within you.' (Luke 17:21) It's that place where you go through prayer and you can feel God's presence and love. In that space you also feel peace. You may be walking through some heavy trials and tests and yet when you enter into this realm you feel peace and power to walk through anything. You can feel that matchless power and you feel secure.

This is a shift into a consciousness of **total dependence** on God, trusting and knowing that you can truly lean on an arm that will **never** give out. You know the buck stops with God; not man or woman. 'Rock of ages cleft for me, let me hide myself in thee.' This song I heard over and over as a child and now I **understand**. There is a place I can go through prayer, meditating, or just stilling myself and getting in touch with the God that dances on my heart. When I am there. I feel love, assurance, restored, renewed, refueled and I can feel the movement and power of the great 'I AM' in me. It's truly a "privilege" and I am so grateful.

This secret place comes by **revelation**. What will give it to us? The Spirit of Truth within us. The secrets God tells me are not for anybody but me and the ones God tells you are for you. Sacred does mean secret. It is best not to discuss certain things with others especially when it is in its embryonic stage. Protect it like a little plant, let it grow strong as you water it with your loving thoughts and feelings. It reminds me of Mary how she went into the temple daily and "pondered" certain things within her heart. Like Mary, let's consider going into the temple of our own consciousness every day and listen to what it is God would have us do. We can only be blessed when we take time to do this.

How do we enter? Jesus says in Matthew 18:3, 'Become as little children.' Children are forgiving. Children are into the moment, most children are naturally joyful and totally dependent on their parents. They aren't worrying, they're just experiencing. They are just being. Sometimes children don't hear you when you call them because they give their **total** attention to whatever they are engaged in at the moment. Nothing else exists except what they are focusing on in that very moment.

Become as a little child means to practice being in the moment and it also means to surrender. It means surrender your adult self. We are all *children* of God not *adults* of God. And you too have a parent who is both mother and father. This parent is one who really loves you and is always seeking the opportunity to love, guide and heal. Being childlike

6

takes practice. We are so accustomed to being in control and calling the shots. We judge matters with our limited perception and we begin to plan how things are to work out without consulting God.

We always hear, "Let Go and Let God." Once I heard it "Let God and Let Go." This hit a string in my heart. When we let God first, then, we can let go. It's too scary to let go with out seeking God and feeling the presence and power of God first!

To surrender is defined out of the dictionary as: "to give up, to relinquish control." We have all seen those movies where a man has his hands up and he is walking with another man behind his back with a gun. This is symbolic of how we are at times. Sometimes we have to be **forced** to surrender. We are getting better, though. When all ideas are exhausted, and there's nobody home, we come to the conclusion, there's nothing I can do, I have just got to let go. We come to the end of our rope and our hands are burning so badly from holding on so tight that we just have to let the rope go. We find ourselves tumbling in the air; it's scary, we feel so vulnerable and unsure. This is the **Trusting Initiation** — we have to walk through the halls of Trust in order to learn how to trust. David called it the 'valley of the shadow of death.' Remember that a shadow isn't real and that this too shall pass.

This is really a great place to find yourself. As painful as it really is, it is still a marvelous place to be. You become real with yourself and with God. You realize that thing called Life is about your relationship with God. It's about listening to the God within your being and being obedient to what it tells you to do; realizing it is God manifesting himself/herself in your life, world and affairs.

7

One day God gave me these words to bless my world:

"God, manifest your love in my life today."

I began to ponder those words in my heart. As I drove my car, I chanted, "God manifest your love in my life today." The day was so wonderful. I went to Bible class and the old testament became more alive to me than ever before in my life. I rested and I went into a deep rest. I went to dinner with my significant other and I even looked more beautiful. Love covered my skin and it clothed me with a rich glow. Love covered my eyes and I saw beauty in everyone I laid my eyes on. Love manifested through every conversation that I had and I was able to receive so many blessings through networking with other like-minded people that I encountered.

What if we really believed that we could afford to relax? What would life be like if we could really **trust** the process of life? Would we wait until we were backed up against a wall? Or would we practice surrendering moment by moment by moment? Would we stop long enough to enter into that secret place inside of ourselves? It only takes a moment and it's worth making time to do it. Once you do it, everything that you are going forth to do will become easier and more successful.

Now take a deep breath. Affirm, "I can afford to relax." Again, "I can afford to relax." Now close your eyes and say it to your heart, "I can afford to relax."

I am studying *Ageless Mind, Timeless Body*, by Deepak Chopra. He has the perfect name because this brother is deep. In the book he says that many of us have that disease called "In A Hurry." Being in a hurry can be quite unsettling to your psyche and your body. We need to take time to really look at our lives and perhaps re-create a lifestyle that spells balance. We need to tell the truth to ourselves, talk with God about our feelings, fears, concerns, desires and ask that God's will be done. Oh yes! This is the surrender prayer:

"God let your will be done in my life, world and affairs."

I used to be afraid to say, "Let your will be done, Lord." I just thought that maybe God would give me someone I didn't really love. How silly that thought is to me now. The creator who created me certainly knows and desires the very best for me.

I also thought that perhaps I'd have to serve and in that serving somewhere in my mind I attached suffering with it. It seems that I was fed a diet of sacrifice and suffering in the church when I was coming up. As I grew older and studied Jesus — who he was, how he lived, a little of how he thought because his thinking is so infinite — I realized it wasn't about suffering but about loving. The greatest healing balm in my life has been the understanding of his unconditional love.

Then I began to realize that I was not only God's daughter but that I was actually pressed out of the body of God. That made me halt in my tracks and take a look at what I was accepting into this royal life that was bequeathed to me when I became a daughter of God. When you know that God resides inside of your very body, sister, you won't allow people to say just anything to you or around you. You lovingly bless them and continue to bless the environment. You carry the peace inside of you, you carry the love with you. You bring happiness with you. You don't look for love, you realize that **you are the love itself**.

My friend wrote a song entitled *The Magic is You*. The first line is, "What you are looking for, is looking." The line is so powerful. Another way of putting it is, what you are looking for you are looking with. The magic is you, it all begins with loving you and the God within you. The song, *The Greatest Love* says, "I found the greatest love" — where? "Inside of me."

We are God's body. We are one. Everyone's function is important and valuable. Our sisters and brothers who are still sleep don't know that they are important and valuable, but we are ALL cells in the body of God.

Loving your body becomes a function to be done for God's sake. When you are expressing health you are expressing the power of God in your cells. When we are staying in the presence of God, our cells are strengthened and our organs are renewed.

I don't believe that most people are aware that there are really two worlds, the visible one and the invisible world. The invisible world controls the visible one. Understanding the kingdom of God means to understand that there is an invisible realm that we can enter on a mental level. It means to understand that God is omniscient. Omniscient means **all-knowing**; you can trust that God really does know all about your problems, complexities, and secrets. I know that we think we are so complex and intricate especially today with all the psycho-social stuff we've learned in these universities, colleges and seminars and what we hear on television in this decade of talk shows. Yet I want you to consider that God knitted you in your mother's womb (Psalms 139) and that you are inside of the body of God. God really does know how to take care of its own.

As a child you don't know. It's that small self in us that struggles to direct and control. If God doesn't tell us quick enough we begin to do things to help God out and we end up 10 steps behind instead of one forward. Trusting God, means waiting on God. Trusting God means you understand that nobody can have what is yours to have. What is yours knows you and it will come to you. Yes, it will come to your doorstep, sisters, it will come into your home and it will come into your lap, **IF** you seek ye

F I R S T

the kingdom of God and its righteousness. This means you must think right. When you keep your mind full of those things that are lovely, that create a kind and good rapport, you are thinking right. Keep your mind stayed on God and all the wonderful attributes of God. When you think right, you will begin to feel right and then you will surely act and react right!!! Thinking right means a diet of forgiveness daily. It is impossible to think right and hold a grudge against someone simultaneously.

Practice sitting in the silence. Start your period of silence with a prayer to center yourself in the presence of God. Then listen to what God says. God often speaks in the form of a thought. Just be still and observe. Be still and listen.

It says in Psalms 91, 'She that *dwelleth* in the secret place...' Dwell doesn't mean those quick prayers that we do before rushing out to work. Dwelling means praying as we drive on the highway, as we wash dishes, vacuum and stand in the bank line. Dwelling means praising God in advance for what we have asked, knowing that "if we pray believing, surely we shall receive" and that as we are yet praying God has sent forth his angels to do our bidding.

You don't need to please and beg God for anything. It's the Father's pleasure to give you the kingdom. Before you call, God has already answered. The desire comes when the thing is **ready** to be birthed through you.

Chapter III

PRAYER IS: ENTERING THE LAND OF ISNESS

'And whatever you ask in prayer, you will receive, if you have faith.'   (Matthew. 21:22)

My grandfather lived a **life of prayer**. At the age of seven I began tuning into his prayers. When he prayed there was a stirring in my being. He was a deacon in the church and whenever he prayed, the spirit of God would swoop down in the sanctuary. He loved the Lord and it was expressed in his love, faithfulness, steadfastness and dedication to God. My grandfather taught me how to pray, not in an instructive way, but because of the love he expressed to me, our family, and our community. I **beheld** Christ in him. I accepted the gift of **living prayer** from him.

I was blessed to have spent time with my grandfather's father about 6 months prior to his transition. He was 107 years old. When pain rattled his frail body, he **praised** the Lord. He praised God that he could **feel**; not feel good or bad but **feel** period. This gift of praising God I embodied and it has really blessed my life.

Prayer is an act of communion (common union) with God. The land of isness **IS** the kingdom of God. This is where this communion takes place. 'The Kingdom of God is within us,' Jesus says. The Kingdom is that place inside where we meet the indwelling Christ. It is not a physical location. When we pray, we enter into the realm where all the health, love, wealth, peace and **all solutions** exist. We feel relieved, encouraged and renewed. We feel God's assurance. He or she that dwelleth in the secret place of the most high, **shall** abide under the SHADOW of the All-mighty.

To dwell means to be there for a substantial period of time. Some of us just "visit" and we haven't made a dwelling place in God where we are conscious of God day and night. As we **dwell** in that place, God says, 'I will **overshadow** your life in the physical realm. I will overshadow you at work, at home and wherever you go... there I AM.' The kingdom of God is within you. Our Brother told us that, and this kingdom is not visible. **It is a state of consciousness.** When we are in real tight spots we enter this kingdom on a very direct route. We come to a point in our lives where we can not see a way and things look hopeless, THEN, we decide to go to God. We pray until we know that we know that we know that God most certainly has heard our requests.

Man has always prayed. Man was pressed out of the body of God and it is an innate impulse for the created to commune with the Creator. From the christian standpoint, prayer originated with Enosh. Genesis 4:26 says, 'Seth also had a son, he named him Enosh.' At that time men began to call on the name of the Lord. The first recorded religion involved in prayer and still being practiced today is Hinduism. Hinduism came about thousands of years ago, before Moses, Buddha and Christ lived.

Prayer is the complete surrender of self. It's important that you consciously realize that there are two worlds — the invisible world and the visible world — and that we live in both **simultaneously**. The invisible world is the "real" world. The invisible world is where the real power is. What is seen comes from what is not seen.

As we enter within and become consciously aware that God is **all-powerful, all-knowing, and everywhere present;** we start at a point of power. We then take our attention off of the so-called problems and place it on God only. We begin then to feel our oneness with God. This realization of oneness empowers us. God is not someplace in the sky but a present help and closer than hands and feet. We are no longer aware of surroundings or our body. We realize that we don't even know what to ask for. And oh, what a blessing to just come into this presence and to understand that we can just bring all of our concerns to the Great One and leave them there! Oh, what a blessing it is to be able to strip naked before God and show him where we are hurting. As we reveal our wounds and share our concerns and pain, God takes them and transforms the situation, circumstance or person and gives it back to us healed, renewed and/or fixed.

Prayer is a means through which God's grace performs its miracles in our experience. *The Revealing Word* by Charles Fillmore says: "Grace came through Jesus Christ. Jesus did a mighty work in establishing for the race a new and higher consciousness in the earth. We can enter into this consciousness by faith in Him and by means of the inner spirit of the law that He taught and practiced."

Grace is **unearned** blessings. God's grace is God's love **pouring out** into our life, world and affairs. When we pray, our consciousness shifts into the place where Grace can easily find entry into our lives. Just as there are many different occasions for prayer, there are also many types of prayer.

The Prayer of Invocation:

To invoke means to "call on." The prayer of invocation calls on the Spirit of God to come into the room. This prayer sets the tone and attitude for worship.

The Prayer of Praise:

This directs the attention of those praying to positive, divine attributes of Joy. As we rejoice and think on what is good, good expands. This type of prayer is rejuvenating and healing. In my opinion, it is the highest form of prayer.

The Prayer of Supplication:

This the most commonly used type of prayer. Many feel that the only way we can have our prayers answered is to **beg** God. We devise prayers that confess to God our unworthiness to receive and then we beg for the answer to be given to us anyway. This method is confusing.

The Prayer of Benediction:

This prayer releases from a ritual domain. It serves to extend the orientation achieved in ritual to the world beyond.

Affirmative Prayer:

Those who practice affirmative prayer understand that they do not have to beg and plead with God. They understand that they are Children of God and they come to God as if they are coming to their loving mother or loving father. They know that there is only One Life and that we are one with the One Life. Affirmative prayer is about conscious recognition of what is. Since there is only One Life and we are all part of that One Life, the person praying recognizes this truth, speaks the word and gives thanks knowing the word she speaks is becoming flesh even as she speaks.

Prayer doesn't change God's mind; it changes our mind, our attitude, our disposition and our beliefs. In this process circumstances change. Prayer connects us to the pervading reality that God is all there is. Pray for everyone, for we are ONE in the body of God. As we become whole, the entire sonship becomes whole.

The Model Prayer....THE LORD'S PRAYER
(Matthew 6: 9-13, Luke 11: 2-4)

This prayer is the Model prayer and can't be duplicated. The disciples asked Jesus to teach them to pray and this is the prayer that was taught to them.

OUR FATHER

the highest authority given to patriarchs during Jesus' time. Our Father doesn't mean gender for God is not male nor female, God is Spirit.

WHICH ART IN HEAVEN

which art everywhere; equally present at the same time. There is no spot where God is not at any time. In Luke 17:21 Jesus says, 'The Kingdom of God is within you.' Heaven is within every one of us. This Kingdom within is not material.

HALLOWED BE THY NAME

The Hebrew culture gave their children names that had a meaning. The African culture did also. These names expressed the **nature** of the child. The name of a thing speaks of its nature, and God's nature is "hallowed." Hallowed means "to make whole." It is God's nature to make things and people whole.

THY KINGDOM COME

Your kingdom is with me, let it be visible in my thoughts, feelings, words, actions and my reactions. Thy kingdom is coming through your children everywhere. We see your vision and we express it as much as we can in our homes, churches, places and work and how we treat others.

THY WILL BE DONE IN EARTH, AS IT IS IN HEAVEN

Your will is being done, for you are **sovereign** on the earth, in the heavens and in the entire universe. I am hooking my will into your will, God. Your will is absolute good for that is what you are.

GIVE US THIS DAY OUR DAILY BREAD

Bread represents "divine substance." Faith is the substance of things hoped for. All of our good is shaped out of Substance (faith). Thank you God that Divine Substance is sufficient each and every day.

AND FORGIVE US OUR DEBTS, AS WE FORGIVE OUR DEBTORS

We are ONE. We only give unto ourselves. People only mirror back to us our own stuff. There is really only one person to forgive...YOU! As we learn to be loving, gentle and non-judgmental to ourselves we will do likewise unto others.

AND LEAD US NOT INTO TEMPTATION, BUT DELIVER US FROM EVIL

God, you are all-powerful and all-knowing; therefore, we ask that you remind us of this truth when thoughts of lack, limitation and fear try to crop up from within. Help us to remember that it's not your will that we be tempted to believe that evil is more powerful than you. Deliver us from false beliefs and fears that we have allowed to live in our minds too long.

FOR THINE IS THE KINGDOM, AND THE POWER, AND THE GLORY, FOREVER

All belongs to God. God is all powerful and gloriously eternal.

AMEN.

It is done!

God will back it up!!!

CHAPTER IV

UNDERSTANDING THE POWER OF THE MIND

'Be not conformed to this world, but be ye transformed by the renewing of your mind.' (Romans 12:2)

This is where I begin. In every workshop or seminar this is where I begin, with the mind. It is essential that you understand what the mind is and how it works. This is the laboratory in which we develop all relationships, the quality of our health, and the quality and texture of our entire lives.

It always stirs the curiosity when I ask, "Where is the Mind located?" Some reply, "It's the brain!" "Is it?," I smile." "Is the mind an organ, can someone perform surgery and take out a mind?" This always brings it home. The mind isn't tangible.

God is mind, Divine Mind. There is only one mind in all the universe. That mind is the mind of God. That mind is your mind. Nothing can be apart from God. The sun and the sunbeam can never be separated. The sunbeam may "act" like it is separate from the sun, but without the sun it wouldn't be a reality at all. We are an idea in the mind of God and we think into God's mind when we think. When we think negative thoughts we are hooking those negative thoughts up with all the power that there is . If we think negative or positive, Mind doesn't judge it, it just does it.

Regardless of how you think and feel from the limited consciousness of your mortal mind, the light of God's mind is shining now in the very depths of your soul, as the perfect pattern, as the true I AM. It will be of no benefit to you until you recognize it and accept it. Only when you embody the reality of YOU will the light spread throughout the subconscious phase of your mind, eliminating darkness and all false beliefs.

Many of us are mentally lazy. We are content with things as they are; we have accepted that this is the way it is and we don't move forward to change things. If you don't have a burning desire to change there will always be an excuse to put things off. Sometimes we have to get to a point where we are just "sick and tired of being sick and tired." Pain is a great motivator.

When you truly get on the spiritual path you will have to come out from under the influences of "race mind" thoughts. Race mind thoughts are the combined thinking of the human race, both conscious and subconscious. That's what Jesus meant when he said, 'Come ye from among them' and 'be ye transformed by the renewing of your mind.'

Let's take sickness for an example. If people believed more in health than in sickness, they would maintain healthier bodies, but most individuals think that it is **normal** for the body to "catch something" or "come down" with something. If you are around people who talk the language of sickness all the time, it may be difficult to protect yourself at times. When they talk their negative talk, just make sure you neutralize it in your own mind. How do you neutralize it? **You neutralize it by putting another positive idea in your mind**. I usually say, "well that's not the truth about **me**."

The same thing holds true when there is constant talk about lack and limitation. 'Come ye from among them and be ye transformed by the renewing of your mind.' Take off those old limiting ideas and pour into your mind the truth! The truth is you are God's expression. God pressed you right out of himself. You and the Father are one. God has already provided for you everything that you could possibly desire and you must decree it to bring it forth into manifestation.

Everything in your life had its beginning in your mind. The Creator loves us so much that this mechanism called "the mind" was established to give us freedom to choose whatsoever we desire. We are choosing all the time with our thoughts, feelings, words, actions and reactions.

Adversity is the result of the incorrect use of our thoughts. God is spirit, we worship God in Spirit and in truth. The whole spirit of God (the Holy Spirit) is already inside of us and our connection comes through the mind. **As a woman thinketh in her heart, so it is in her life**. We pray, we commune with God and God speaks back through our thoughts! God places pictures, visions and thoughts in our mind. We begin to desire to experience what we see in those pictures, visions and thoughts.

The word desire from its etymological origin means "of the father" (*de*: of, *sire*: Father) The Creator slips desires down into our hearts and souls. This process is God's way of saying, "Here's a sneak preview of the life that I planned for you before the foundations of the earth. Now my child, you don't have to try to figure out how this is going to become a manifested reality. Accept that I have placed this desire in your heart and soul and that I (the Most High) within you, **will** make sure that you are always in the right place, at the right time, and doing the right thing. We usually get busy spinning our wheels, giving God outlines and instructions to make things come about. **Stop!** Focus on these ideas:

God is my supply and my supplier.
God is the gift and the giver.
God knows and God shows.

As you think on God, God brings everything together for you. God reads the need on your heart and becomes the thing you need! Allow Spirit to give you the outline, then move in the direction that you are to led to move in. You will be led as you practice being still, praying, listening and then moving your feet.

Our lives are transformed as we keep our minds on God. Peace is established in our minds, thus in our affairs, as we keep our mind on God. As we focus on the nature of God — love, beauty, health and abundance, these things are established in our worlds. **Remember that you must take time to remember who you are each and every day.** Don't leave home without remembering . Remembering who you are allows you to operate from a base of success; you no longer strive for success, you realize that you are **made** out of success for you are made out of God. You live, move and have your being in God, therefore, **you can not fail**.

Psychology has taught us that there are three parts to the mind — the conscious, subconscious and superconscious mind. The conscious mind observes, thinks and evaluates. You are using your conscious mind now as you read. You are thinking, evaluating, and accepting some ideas readily and pondering others. The conscious mind is the part of the mind where we reason, analyze, select, conclude, reject, decide. This is the masculine aspect of the mind, the logical side associated with the intellect.

The subconscious part of the mind is the part that receives the thoughts from the conscious part and goes to work to produce what is thought about. This is the part of the mind that is connected to the Soul. This is the feminine aspect of the mind. There is a divine design for our lives in the soul and it is communicated through the subconscious mind. We are so busy making conscious choices and decisions with such limited knowledge. If we could see from the view of the soul , we would more readily allow God to unfold our lives and we would not have to struggle so much.

The subconscious mind acts just like a robot. It does what you tell it to do and you tell it by what you think and what you feel. Your thinking ability is masculine in nature and your feeling ability is feminine. When you bring them together, **you can create anything**. When you worry, you are telling your subconscious mind to bring about the thing that you are worrying about. **Every thought is a prayer!**

Many beliefs are in the subconscious mind already. If you want to know what is in your subconscious mind, take an honest look at your life. Your life mirrors your subconscious mind. The subconscious mind stores everything, events from your childhood to adulthood. **If you want to change your life, it begins by changing your thinking**.

This process is not easy but it is also not easy to live an unhappy life. You are not really living when you are depressed, unfulfilled, or broke. So many people are so mentally lazy and don't want to do the work. They would prefer that someone give them a magical formula, i.e., burn a candle, do incantations etc. Yet there is a law in operation and as we align with the law positively we see positive results; as we are out of alignment, we experience those results also.

The superconscious is the part of the mind that is the essence of what you really are. Some call this part of the mind the "God" mind. You get assistance from the super-conscious mind when your thoughts are in harmony with love. This part of the mind will not blend in with negativity. When you are thinking negative thoughts you are really out there all alone. This mind is very active during dreams, bringing you ideas, solutions, guidance and instruction through the language of dreams.

Chapter V

THE ATOMIC POWER OF THE SPOKEN WORD

'Heaven and Earth will pass away, but my words will never pass away.' (Mark 13:31)

Webster defines atomic as: "Something considered as an indestructive and irreducible constituent of a specified system... A rapid release of energy...

What is this indestructive and irreducible thing of which Jesus said in Mark 13:31 that "Heaven and Earth will pass away, yet **IT** would by no means pass away"? That **IT** is the word.

Today we use the **word** and the **Bible** interchangeably. The word came in the beginning when there was no Bible, so we are talking about **every word** that proceedeth out of your mouth (Deut. 8:3). **All** of our words are creative.

The Revealing Word by Charles Fillmore says, "The word is the agency by which God reveals himself/herself/Itself in some measure to all men, but to a greater degree to highly developed souls; the word gives order and regularity to the movement of things and is the divine dynamic of God."

Let's consult with John. Get your bible and turn to Chapter 1 verses 1-5.

In the beginning was the Word, and the Word was
with God, and the Word an God.
The same was in the beginning with God.
All things were made by him; and without him was
not anything made that was made.
In him was life; and the life was the light of men.
And the light shineth in darkness; and the darkness
comprehended it not.

Now, let's get an even deeper understanding of this. In Genesis (the word means *beginning*), it repeats the phrase "And God said...,"

"And God said...," "And God said..." God spoke the word **aloud**. And this is important to take note of, for there is a message in this. There wasn't any one else there. Yet God spoke it and it gave off the necessary vibrations to create from the very substance in the atmosphere (the invisible, the ever present substance) and the atoms obeyed and became in the physical everything that God spoke. And we, you and I, were given this same power to create in our life, world and affairs. And yes we use this power all of the time whether we are aware of it or not.

God spoke these words upon the waters (waters symbolize Spirit). Spirit moved upon Itself. We are made out of God and we are 99% water. We can speak the word inside of our own being into our heart and the physical realm will respond just like it did in Genesis Chapter 1.

God made things out of Itself and still makes things out of Itself by some inner act upon Itself. The atomic power of the spoken word sets the law in motion and the result is creation. In the beginning God. In the beginning Spirit. In the beginning intelligence. No manifest universe. Only the **Logos**: the creative word. No planets. No visible form; it was dark and void, and God spoke with the power of 1 billion E.F. Huttons. God said, "Let there be Light" and there was... light. God is God and has the ability to say just "Let there be." Since we are offspring we have that same power.

When we are at the beginning of a new position, new relationship, a new project, a new dream, all we have is an idea. God gives us a **divine key in** Genesis... ask for Light/Divine Guidance — 'Let there be light!'

Now let me warn you, when you speak "Let there be light in this situation, in this relationships, regarding this job etc.," you will surely get the light. This light will not only shine on whatever you are requesting but it will also shine on you. I have spoken, "Let there be light" and wished days later that I could have retracted that request. Be ready for sheer transparency. Ask God for the ability to change. Remember too that at the beginning of any idea there is God waiting to guide, to instruct and reveal matters to you just for the asking.

John goes on to say that "all things" were made through Him. Who is **Him?** Him is the Word. Without the word, nothing was made that was made. The word of God is permanent. That is why Jesus said in Mark 13:31, 'Heaven and Earth shall pass away but my Word shall stand.'

Charles Fillmore in the *Twelve Powers of Man* says, "Among the apostles of Jesus, Phillip represents the power faculty of the mind. The word Phillip means "a lover of horses," horses representing the physical activity, power, "horsepower." The power center in the throat controls all the vibratory energies of the organism. It is the open door between the formless and the formed worlds of vibrations. A connection is made through sound.

That's why the walls came tumbling down around the walls of Jericho. Every word that goes forth receives its specific character from the power faculty. Jesus, through the spoken word, conveyed an inner spiritual quickening that would enter the mind of the recipient and awaken the inactive spirit and life of the person. When a voice has united with the life of the soul, that voice becomes an instrument to be used for healing by the All-mighty Creator himself.

We saw this atomic power loosed in a man named Dr. Martin Luther King. We see the results of his words in the President's cabinet, in the office of Surgeon General, in NASA, and in Mayoral seats throughout the United States.

In the book, *The Millionaire Joshua* by Catherine Ponder she says, "When you speak the word with feeling, you release an atomic power." Many times we speak our affirmations with tongue and cheek. The key is to first become consciously aware of God, to become consciously aware of that presence within you and make a mental and emotional connection first, **then** speak the word. There must be a head and heart connection. The act of speaking the word is an action and action is a masculine principle. Feeling is a feminine principle. When you bring speaking and feeling together you have something that is "whole" and a collective entity that can produce a third thing. The third thing can be a physical baby or the birth of an idea.

Catherine Ponder says that our words can speed up results as much as 80 percent. Our words accelerate activities. **Our words make the atoms change within our cells.** We have access to atomic energy.

We understand the word virtue to mean "pure" and it does. However, the word virtue also means **"the power to produce effects."** We have been pressed out of the body of God, we live in the mind of God, we are told that "in God we live, move and have our being."

The spirit of God hovered over Mary's womb and

30

impregnated her to bring forth the Word. This Word became flesh and it dwelt among us. We too often hear that women are not to deliver the word in certain churches, yet, the fact is **she gave birth to the Word**! Why can't she speak something whose very essence came from her? That's the most ridiculous thing I've ever heard. Think about it.

In Job 22:28 it says, 'Thou shalt decree a thing and it shall be established unto you.' We have the power to produce specific effects and we can do this via the spoken word. Along with speaking the word aloud we must feel these words and think on the desired results. All words create. We are creating all the time. In some of the most casual conversations we are still creating.

I saw Oprah Winfrey when she interviewed Maya Angelou. Maya said, "Words get into your clothes, the furniture and the environment and they become alive." She doesn't allow people to speak negatively in her presence at all. It takes courage to stop people from speaking negatively in our presence.

My friend who is an African Priestess shared from her culture the word "Afroshé," which means the ability to speak utterances and produce results. We call this same process an **affirmation**. An affirmation is a positive statement of truth about who we really are. Who we really are is Spiritual beings whose perfection is still intact. No matter what we've experienced, there is a part of us that is untouched, unaffected and whole. As we speak words of truth this perfected state becomes more visible to ourselves and others.

The spiritual woman is acutely aware of her words and takes time to correct her sentences once she realizes she has spoken something that she really doesn't want to come true in her experience. When I realize I've said something that I really don't want to experience I cancel it out by saying "Cancel, cancel, love, love." It's like canceling an order because my words are creative and powerful and I've seen too many times how quickly they can manifest.

The spiritual woman knows that she was been "spiritually adopted" and is now an heir of God. She has entered into a supernatural life. It doesn't matter what the appearances are; she knows that she can see beyond the appearances and see the perfection in any situation. She doesn't judge by appearance. The master teacher Jesus tells her that this is possible. When he saw the man with a withered hand, he didn't see the withered hand, he saw the perfected hand, and he too spoke the word that became a reality.

When the appearance of sickness comes, the spiritual woman speaks the word and speaks the word until the realization comes forth that there is no sickness in the Spiritual realm of which we are a part of. As she is steadfast in her **belief**, healing takes place outwardly. Sometimes one's transition or death is a healing. I remember praying with a friend who had cancer. She was asking for deliverance and within 7 days she died. Some would say God didn't answer the prayer, yet God did. She was delivered and is now free.

Sharon, a member of our support group, gave us a beautiful example about the power of the word. "My son was ill in the middle of the night. I wasn't home at the time, because I was baby-sitting for a friend. I heard the telephone ringing about 3:00 a.m. I couldn't get to it in time, yet intuitively I knew to call home. My son answered the phone, saying, "Mom I need to go to the hospital, I am in so much pain." He explained that there was a lump in his groin area and he was sobbing. As I looked at the clock, I realized I didn't have my car there, there was ice on the street and a baby who was asleep.

All I could think to do was to pray. I became very still and said, "God, God who is everywhere, God who is **all**-powerful, God who is **all**-knowing my child is in trouble, tell me what to do, Lord please fix this situation." In my mind I was seeing this lump dissolving and I was imagining that when I called back, he would tell me that everything was ok. When I called back he said, "Mom the pain is gone, I think that I can go to sleep now."

All words create. Words have life. Words are containers; they carry life. Instead of fretting, worrying and fearing, practice speaking the word. The following decrees are very powerful when spoken aloud with conviction and feeling seven times. If you are unable to speak them aloud, read them to yourself with feeling.

Speaking the word for…

…A NEW POSITION

I believe that there is a divine position that is just perfect for me. This position is seeking me right now and it finds me. I am qualified for this position and I am happy in it. I now accept this position; it comes in a divine way and the pay is divine. The location and hours are perfect. I now release this truth into the universe and I wait in joyful anticipation that it is done now!!!

…DIVINE WORK

The purpose of my life is now manifesting into the perfect position for me. My work is so rewarding and unbelievably fulfilling. My work environment is peaceful, interesting and I find it easy to be productive. My work is organized and I approach large projects with ease, peace, clarity and a spirit of cooperation. I attract cooperative, understanding and supportive team players.

...INCREASE IN INCOME

I am receiving an substantial increase in income; it exceeds my expectations! It well exceeds all of my financial commitments and I always have plenty to spare and to share. I tithe, fulfill my financial obligations, share with others, invest and I have a whole lot of fun!

...CHANGE

A divine plan is unfolding, one that lovingly guides me to my good. In spite of myself I hear, I understand and I move with the mighty spirit of God leading, guiding and protecting. Divine ideas take hold in mind and they unfold in my life quickly and in God's grace. The presence of divine order permeates my world and all is well.

...DIVINE HUSBAND

In the heart inside of my heart I know that my divine husband already exists and I thank God that he joins us in love, peace, and God's amazing grace. I do not seek out, I seek in and we come together in God's way and timing. Our marriage becomes a blessing for everyone who knows us. Thank you and it is so now!

...PROSPERITY

I am one with all the wealth that there is in this universe right now. I focus my attention on God's abundance and abundance moves into my life, world and affairs in unexpected and expected ways. I now experience abundance in the form of money, right relationships, joyful experiences, health and happiness.

...HEALING FOR YOUR CHILD

My child belongs to God. I now behold God in my child expressing as my child. I see with my spiritual eye God's healing energy, touching my child's mind, body, emotions, actions and reactions. I let go and let our loving Father/Mother God take control. I see only God and therefore I see only good!

...FINANCIAL SELF-SUFFICIENCY

I live in an abundant universe and I recognize myself right now as a self-sufficient being. Life is infinite and eternal and life is always sufficient to supply needs. Divine substance expresses in my life, world and affairs as divine self-sufficiency at all times and forever.

...IN-LAWS

I forgive myself for any unkind thought, word and deed that I have directed towards them. I forgive them for the same. I behold God in them. I now release all past negativity. Guilt, condemnation and blame no longer have a hold on me. I release them to their highest good. I am free and they are free too.

...RELEASING THE PAST

I no longer brood over the past. Brooding is just an excuse to stay where I am. All people of the past have been teachers for me. Some taught me how not to be, and some, how to be. This now moment is all that counts. For the thoughts I think in this moment create my future and now is all that I have.

...GRIEF

There is one life and that life is eternal. God's love is enfolding me and comforting me. I now realize that I can still communicate with my loved one, for spirit never dies. God is removing all heaviness and attachment from me so that I can freely let go and let my loved one experience another mansion.

Infinite Intelligence and Wisdom goes before me and my trip is safe and enjoyable. I let go of all anxiety and relax in the omnipresence of God. Where ever I go I know God is there, for there is no spot where God is not.

...DIVORCE

The love of God permeates my mind, heart and spirit through this process. I surrender all judgment of myself and my spouse. I cease talking negatively about my spouse, in-laws or myself. I give thanks for the growth that I am experiencing in this process.

Chapter VI

RELATIONSHIPS

*For your Maker is your husband — Lord Almighty
is his name. (Isaiah 54:5)*

Relationships can not be successful until we find the courage and **make** the time to examine our childhoods. It can be scary. We've spent most of our lives appearing as if we have it all together. The process which we'll explore at the end of this chapter isn't easy, yet it's **imperative!** I remember when I took the plunge. Mangled, tired and bewildered, yet I took the plunge. I was tired of waiting for the prince to come in a BMW to come and drive me away into paradise. I was mangled inwardly from the unresolved pain of living in a home where verbal and physical abuse was the **norm** rather than the exception. I was bewildered not knowing if I'd ever find a space of resolution or a period of contentment.

I found a "gentle" therapist who helped me to look back in my childhood. It was a lot of work and I was terrified. I kept feeling like I was going to discover something within so terrible, so frightening, so powerfully controlling that I'd be consumed. I did get in touch with some powerful, frightening stuff, but it didn't hurt me. It set me free.

I, like so many women of color, thought that psycho-therapy was for rich white folk; however, I know better now. It is a viable and valuable way for us to look into our souls and understand what is there, how it got there, and how to let it go.

As children, our caregivers transfer their experience on to us. Consciously and unconsciously, according to our perceptions of what we saw and experienced as children, we re-create what we saw, heard and lived. We draw people into our lives over and over again who mirror the relation-ships we had with our caregivers and the relationship they had with each other.

In *Creative Visualization* Shakti Gawain says, "The people we are in relationship with are always a mirror reflecting our own beliefs and simultaneously we are mirrors reflect-ing their beliefs."

In Alice Miller's book *For Your Own Good*, she analyzes Hitler's childhood as the source of the cruelty he inflicted on others. Hitler had a sadistic father who also had a stepfather who beat him into a state of unconsciousness many times. Hitler watched his mother being beaten. He began to take pride in the number of lashes he could take without making a sound. How many times have we heard parents whip chil-dren and say, "That doesn't hurt you!" No wonder we're so confused. This is of course no excuse for what Hitler or many of us do as adults. It is, however, easy to see why many of us are confused about what we do and do not **feel** in our relationships.

Sometimes the pain of our childhood is too painful to remember. The mind won't allow certain memories to sur-face until we are ready to deal with certain events. Ironically, it's the pain that gets us ready.

About 15 years ago I was **ready**... dissatisfied to the bone. I read a book entitled *Woman Awareness* by Ann Meyers. There were several exercises in the book which really tapped into some events that had been tucked away in my memory. These events came back to my remembrance while processing. For example, when I was 12 my male cousin urinated on me while I was napping one afternoon. As I was lying on the beach in Mexico this experience came back vividly in my mind and I let out a scream.

How could I have forgotten that? Maybe that's why I'd been carrying around a feeling of being "p——ed on." The mind has that ability to tuck things away so tight and secure until we're no longer consciously aware of it. Maybe this is what grace really is. Yet, the stuff is still in there very much alive and affecting our lives and relationships every day.

On about my third visit to the therapist, I realized for the first time in my 35 years that I was angry with my Mother. We were tight, I could talk to her about most anything, but the hidden anger was still there. I consciously knew I was mad as h—- at my Dad, because he was so controlling, violent and oppressive.

During therapy, I was taken back in memory to my childhood experience and I began ranting and raving, "Why did you allow us to experience Daddy's brutality? Why didn't you leave? Why couldn't you protect us? Why did you whip me when I went for help?" You talk about something messing up your head — you get beaten by your Mom for soliciting help because she's being beaten!

Why hadn't I realized I was angry with my Mother before today?, I asked. My therapist replied, "Your Mother is your God as a child, and you don't get mad at God!" I worked very diligently and I forgave them both. This therapeutic experience helped me to realize how wounded they were and how they had no idea that they were wounding me. I was able to see them as little children in my mind's eye and to see their pain, love them, and tuck them away in my heart. This process was invaluable to me. If you feel seeking support is a weakness, rethink that thought. This process created a **shift** in my mind, thus in my perception of them, which was the beginning of some deep inner healing and the beginning of a **new** relationship with both of my parents.

A part of me wanted to go to my parents to discuss things that I discovered. However, I'd already had the experience of going to my parents to discuss things that went on in my childhood and they didn't have a clue about what I was talking about. I see people do that all the time and get so frustrated. The frustration comes because the person is expressing their perception of what happened and often times the other person with whom they had the experience with perceives the exact same experience in a totally different way. I'd already grown enough to realize that we can all experience the same event and we can all experience it differently, **and to let that be ok.**

At this point it wasn't important to tell my Mother and Father off, it was important that I mend. Writing and journaling my feelings were invaluable for me. If you're ready to find the broken places, get a notebook and begin by answering the following questions. Make sure that you've set aside about 3 hours to really go within quietly and uninterrupted. Writing exposes the suppressed pain and disappointment to the light and its powerful grip subsides. **Get it out on paper.** It loses its power when you get it on the outside of you and look at it. You don't have to share this information with anyone. If you decide that you would like to share and there's a non-judgmental, trusting person in your life you may want to share what you've discovered doing these exercises. Use another sheet of paper if you need more room to fully explore your **feelings**.

ಇ

Describe the qualities you liked about your mother or caregiver.

_____

_____

_____

_____

_____

Describe the qualities you disliked about your mother or caregiver.

_____

_____

_____

_____

_____

Describe the qualities you liked about your father or care-giver.

_____

_____

_____

_____

Describe the qualities you disliked about your father or caregiver.

_____

_____

_____

_____

Describe in detail your relationship with mother (or care-giver).

_____

_____

_____

_____

Describe in detail your relationship with father (or caregiver).

_____

_____

_____

_____

Describe your "feelings" if mother and/or father were absent.

_____

_____

_____

_____

Describe the relationship between mother and father. How did the relationship make you feel?

_____

_____

_____

_____

_____

How much do you know about your parents' history?
Describe their history in as much detail as possible.

_____

_____

_____

_____

Next... make yourself a chart like the one below. You will start with the first person you ever dated and end with the most recent person you've experienced.

This exercise is so valuable because you get an opportunity to "see" the pattern. It gets revealed through this exercise. Certain issues continue to come up, certain themes. These themes are more important than the people. Remember people just mirror out your beliefs. Complete the following data for each person you have dated. Start with your first boyfriend.

Name of boyfriend	*Why I was attracted*	*Why we broke up*

Characteristics you liked and disliked.

_____

_____

_____

_____

_____

_____

_____

Review what you've written about your parents' character-istics. Is there a correlation with this data and one you've just written about your more intimate relationships? What's that correlation?

_____

_____

_____

_____

_____

_____

_____

_____

My relationship with my Mother was loving and warm. Mother was unhappy a lot. She was economically dependent and she was emotionally and physically abused. I took on a role as her "protector."

My relationship with my Father was distant. I was afraid of him. For many years I prayed that he would die. I even planned a few times to kill him myself. After many years of self-exploration, self-assessments and healing from the Holy Spirit, I realize that my Father was hurting too and he just expressed his anger towards the closest people to him, his family.

The energy between my Mother and Father was strained. I was programmed with their beliefs, actions and words. The following themes rippled through their conversations to me, to each other, to friends. These are the messages my tape recorder (my subconscious mind) recorded.

"All men are the same...no good!"

"You can't trust a man!"

"All men cheat!"

"Women have no power!"

"Men have the fun, women have depression."

"You must keep girlfriends at a distance, don't tell them your business, especially about you and your man."

I remember when I was 17 years old being so shut down. My best friend and her Mother said I was just mean because of my piercing silence with a boyfriend. I wasn't mean, I was **paralyzed**. I was frozen! I didn't talk to him because I

DIDN'T KNOW HOW TO. In my house, they didn't talk. There was mostly silence or arguments. I felt unworthy. I was afraid and I believed he'd be unfaithful because that's what men did, and in the end, he was unfaithful. It was a self-fulfilling prophecy. But I was not ready to deal with my sickness at that point. It would be 11 years later when I'd realize I just had to get well.

I grew up in the church. Literally from the age of 4 I was in church sometimes for 3 services on Sunday. I was programmed to do the right thing and told what would happen to me if I did not. I did most of it naturally anyway. At the age of 17 I got married to get away from home. I was adventurous and rebellious. The marriage, which was illegal because I forged my father's signature, didn't last a year. I was married, miserable, afraid and guilt-ridden. Before I left my husband, I went to see my grandparents. It was like sitting before the King and Queen of life. I had to hear all their beliefs about women who leave their husbands, what God wanted me to do, and how I had made my bed hard and now had to sleep in it. I listened. I cried. I felt condemned. I was a failure. I was doomed. My physical Gods had just doomed me to hell.

After dinner one evening, I announced to my husband that I was miserable and felt like I needed some space. I told him I was leaving. He began to throw things around the apartment. I grabbed my coat fully aware that the next thing he would throw would be me. He reached for me as I was going out of the door and missed my coat by an inch. I ran to a neighbor's house. I had no clothes and no money. "Lord, what do I do now?" I sobbed. The next day, after I had calmed down, I called Sara, the owner of the modeling agency I had been working for. She told me to take cab, she'd pay the fare and that I could stay with her.

No clothes, no money yet I knew I wasn't going home. I cried and worried and finally I decided I would stop eating and just waste away. I quit my job because I was afraid my husband would come there and beat me. I began wasting. My friend Sara worried with me and about me. She tried to give me advice but I couldn't hear her.

After two weeks, she told me that a mutual friend of ours wanted to talk to me. The friend lived a few doors away from where I had lived, and my husband still lived. I had seen him coming and going, but I knew very little about him. The one thing I knew from observation, rumor and Sara, was that he was wealthy.

When Sara invited him, he came over a few times. He and I spent time talking and laughing. As I discovered that I liked him, I immediately moved into conflict. My religious upbringing and the fact that I was still married placed me in quite a dilemma. The truth is, he came into my life at a time when I was very vulnerable and weak. I was game, but I was weak. Today, he could be called a lover. Back then he was a friend who took me shopping for clothes and out to dinners, parties and the like.

He offered me money for an apartment which scared me half to death. I was too afraid to shack up because I thought my parents would disown me. He gave me cash to pay one year's rent on a townhouse and he kept his own apartment. He bought me a new car and he paid for my divorce. I couldn't figure out if he was God or the Devil. I knew that he had rescued me for awhile and that was all that mattered at that time.

The relationship did not last because I got bored with the "stuff" he bought and he became very possessive. I didn't mind being taken care of, but I would not be owned. I stayed for 1 year and I knew I had to get out of that situation too. When I told him that I wanted out he pulled his 45 pistol out and placed it to the temple of my head. I didn't flinch and I wasn't afraid, I was numb. I really didn't care if he pulled it or not. I was living in such isolation and misery with so much stuff that I already felt dead. When he realized how numb and how much pain I was really in, he cried and he said, "I love you so much, you know there's nothing I won't do for you, but if you are that miserable, leave. I'll still help you until you can get on your feet." I left and moved to Detroit with some distant relatives.

This should have been down time for me. This should have been the time I took to search my soul and get myself together. I wasn't strong enough to search my soul and I did not know I needed to be fixed. I always thought falling in loved fixed you. I was still thinking at that time that loneliness only meant being alone by yourself.

So, I fell in love and got married, again. This time, my world, my every thought revolved around my husband. When I had our son, I just knew I had gone to heaven. I did not realize how truly sick I was emotionally. I was very insecure and jealous. I couldn't bear for him to be close with other women. I was uncomfortable with my beauty, sexuality and ultimately with my life. I did not know that the pain of my childhood was a wound still festering inside of me. I wasn't conscious of the pain, but it was **active** and it was manifesting throughout my life.

I was married to a wonderful man, yet he had many of my father's characteristics, namely the inability to deal with intimacy — and I don't mean sex. Intimacy means revealing yourself allowing yourself to be emotionally naked with your partner. Some people never feel safe enough to do that. I understood it then and I understand it now, yet my soul longed for it.

49

He was wounded too. We really thought we could heal each other. We didn't know that we were entering the **"Twilight Zone"** where all of my past programming from my parent, grandparents and experiences would join with all of his. The joining brought up so many issues in the marriage. We had a beautiful home, new cars every two years, winters in the Caribbean or Mexico, a boy for him and a girl for me, a maid 5 days a week. I shopped, traveled, entertained and was as miserable as I could be.

I felt that I should have been able to make it with someone everyone loved, someone who was kind, pretty considerate, good-looking and a great provider. Many people felt and said I had it all and I struggled thinking, "Darn, you got it all and you still aren't happy. Something **must** be wrong with you." A statement that an old boyfriend said to me played in my mind often, "You're just a misfit. You don't belong anywhere. Some people are just born misfits in life and you just happen to be one of them." I began to believe that I was one of those people.

I was looking for the answer in clothes, trips, parties, sex, money, influential friends and it wasn't to be found in any of it because the answer was inside of me. We loved each other so much, yet we couldn't make the marriage happen. We were both too wounded to allow it to happen.

Thomas Merton, author of *Love and Need: Is Love a Package or a Message?* explains the way we are programmed by capitalistic society through the electronic media. "Love is regarded as a deal. The deal presupposes that we all have needs which have to be fulfilled by means of exchange. In order to make a deal you have to appear in the market with a worthwhile product, or if the product is worthless, you can get by if you dress it up in a good-looking package. We unconsciously think of ourselves as objects for sale on the market. In doing this we come to consider ourselves and others not as **persons** but as **products...** as 'goods' or in other words, as packages."

If you look at the Soaps, it's all about deals. Women were treated legally as chattel, less than humans, and many sisters feel like objects because they have bought into the capitalistic programming. We look at packages instead of looking at hearts, spirits and souls. I understand what recovering alcoholics and addicts mean when they say they are grateful they became alcoholics because of what they've been able to discover in recovery. Well, I am grateful for the pain that made me attempt suicide in many ways. Today I know I really didn't want to die, I really wanted to live and I was dying, drowning in opulence, emptiness , denial and lies.

Waking up from the dream of hell into the life I really wanted and now realized I could create, caused vast change for me and impacted my marriage, home, friends and environment. I no longer enjoyed being around certain types of people. The social scene bored me and it was such an integral part of my husband's work and life. I finally made a decision to stop going out with him socially. I became detached. I began thinking unlimited and sounding like a space cadet to many people including my husband. When my husband introduced me to others sometimes he'd preference the introduction with, "Man, my wife is really nice, she's just a little different."

I had prayed so much for our marriage to heal. Many ministers, famous and unknown, prayed for us. We were anointed, we went to counseling, we surrendered and we prayed. One night I saw an exit sign in my bedroom and it was a purple neon color. Many times I was instructed to go and I was too afraid. I was dependent on my husband. I wanted to be protected and taken care of like a child. I really enjoyed the time I had to cultivate my relationship with God and while my husband was out in the world making the provisions which provided me the opportunity to do that, I felt that I **owed** him.

I acquired many illnesses that were traced back to one thing — **unhappiness.** But I still couldn't figure out what to do. Fear literally immobilized me. A friend told me that when I didn't need to ask anyone anymore questions about whether to stay or leave, I would know **exactly** what to do. That day surely came. It ain't over until it's over is so true.

I came to understand that my husband and I were **spiritual** beings who chose the path of marriage for the purpose of our soul's growth. We weren't consciously aware of it when we got married nor were we fully conscious of it at the time we parted. In meditation one day Spirit showed me a reflection of us bandaged from head to toe. Spirit instructed us to pray daily as we moved through this process of coming apart so that the tear wouldn't be so severe. We prayed and we treated each other very tenderly and gently. Our relationship became so sweet and tender that at times I thought we could make it. Yet it became real clear to both of us that we could not.

I knew that just getting another husband wasn't the answer, because with my healed mind I knew my husband wasn't the problem. It was my beliefs that needed to be healed. I could marry 50 men and none of them would work until I became whole and healed from the core. I am still healing today. The difference is that I'm much stronger. Practice makes perfect. A figure skater practices daily and goes to the Olympics after several years. Well, now I am ready to go the Olympics, that's the difference.

How does one begin? Begin by doing those exercises I

gave you previously. Take the time to honestly see how the relationships your parents had or caregivers had coincide with the relationships you've been having.

I believe it's easier to see if you look at the themes, because looking at the themes separates all the personal opinions. For instance, my themes were cheating, possessiveness, and insecurity. These themes existed in my home and in my relationships. Instead of saying, "Jake's a —————." I look at the theme and I am able to separate the person from the theme. It really isn't about Jake, it's about me. **It's always about me.** Jake, John, Joe or Pete is only the bringer of the theme, presenting it to me to be healed. They are **mirrors.** Boy, does that shift your perception on your past relationships. Take some time to think this through for in it there is healing, freedom and salvation (saving you from years of guilt, blaming, judging and getting nowhere).

When problems arise in my relationships, it's about me going within and asking myself some honest questions and not accepting anything but an honest answer from myself. We can't change people. We can ask ourselves what are the benefits we're receiving from the relationships, we can look at whether we are growing or not. Is it nurturing me? Is it peaceful? Is it a loving relationship? Am I giving and receiving? Am I giving only? Am I receiving only? Am I loving myself?

Do I love myself? We are so quick to say yes. Yet, our bodies, homes, lifestyles tell us just how much we are loving ourselves. Own the truth about where you are at any given moment. Own it and stop trying to cover up stuff — **it is whatever it is.** It's not to be judged, just understood and when we just become willing for a "change" to take a place, our willingness is the key that turns on the Power to assist us in that change.

Not only can you not change others, you can't even change yourself! If you could have, you would have lost those 20 lbs. ten years ago and you would have stopped smoking when you quit 3 years ago. Until we acknowledge that we are powerless to improve ourselves and recognize that there is a Higher Power, it's a vicious, unending, non-victorious struggle. When you admit your shortcomings and surrender them to the Higher Power, you're opening yourself up to Omnipotence — the All power — and it begins to move on your brain frequency. It moves on your thoughts and manipulates your behavior to a point that you're not even consciously aware of. I remember how many times I had surrendered red meat. I had come to believe through research that it was harmful for me and I had been eating it all of my life. I kept saying I was willing to give it up but it took almost 7 years before I cut back from eating it 80% of the time to 5% of the time.

And I don't consciously know when it happened. When we surrender a thing and **keep surrendering and being willing for the change** to occur, it does. When the Higher Power is creating the change, it's gentle, it's without effort or struggle. It's done for you, around you, through you and as you.

In your forgiveness process, first just being **willing** to forgive a person is important. I had to forgive a man who molested me and it was very difficult. That's why I understand it when workshop participants come and say, "But Linda, you just don't understand, you don't know what that person did, you can't forgive that!" Believe me, I understand. Nevertheless, it **can** be done and not only can it be done, it **must** be done. **Just be willing.** I kept writing "I forgive James Doe for what he did and he forgives me and we are both free to experience the highest good that the

Universe has for us now!" I was writing it and affirming it, but in my heart I still didn't feel it. However, I persisted, and finally one day **I did feel it** and I was granted an opportunity to come face to face with this person a few weeks before be died. He was blind at this time. I had compassion for him. I embraced him and I felt the Love of God flow from my heart to him and he died a few weeks later. I freed myself and him. I felt so good. It was such a healing experience. I realize that I couldn't experience my good as freely and abundantly as I desired with this skeleton hanging in my closet.

A truth teacher once told me that when you don't forgive others, everyone you haven't forgiven is on an invisible chain and you drag them around with you wherever you go. During a meditation I was shown how unforgiveness builds an invisible wall keeping out all your good.

Chapter VII

ATTRACTING YOUR DIVINE WORK

'Where your treasure is, there your heart will be also.'   (Matthew 6:21)

We have all been blessed with gifts, talents and abilities. I know some people will say, "I don't know where my gifts are." Sometimes gifts are not recognized because they are done so easily and they are sort of second nature. Your gift, that thing that you do so naturally, is the key to unleash the treasures that have been so eagerly awaiting their manifestation. In my training experiences I have experienced many people who say "I don't know what my special gift is." I have actually felt the same way myself. Arnold Patent, author of *You Can Have It All*, teaches people to do what they love and the money will follow.   If you can do something that not **all** people can do, it is a gift. Begin sharing your gift today. **Listening is a gift** — everyone doesn't have the capacity to be a good listener. I am a good listener and it was through a workshop experience that I really realized that was a gift. **Caring for others is a gift** — everyone doesn't have the ability to care. **Creating humor is a gift** — laughter is truly medicine.

There is a divine design or divine plan for your life and since there really is a divine design for your life there is also divine work for you to do that only **you** can do. Our desires are our **previews** of the soul.

In Marianne Williamson's book, *A Return To Love,* she says, "Don't ask God to send you a brilliant career, ask Him to show you the brilliance that is within you." It is the recognition of your brilliance that releases it into expression. As we focus on what is good within us and what we really enjoy doing, **because of the law of mind action,** (thoughts held in mind produce after their kind) we will be presented with opportunities to express those qualities. No matter what we do, **we are all here to minister**. No matter what form our job or activity takes, we are actually channels for God to express through and we actually **start** from success. You are made out of God-stuff, Genesis says you were made in the image and likeness of God.

You really work for God, Inc. Your title — Ambassador of Love. The salary is unlimited. Your benefits are perfect health, bonuses, vacations, unexpected and undreamed of blessings, security for the rest of this life. The top benefit is eternal life. Working for God, Inc. is like being in the service, you have to wait for your orders to find out where you are going next.

I attended a workshop in the early eighties, facilitated by Arnold Patent. The exercises we experienced were very powerful. The workshop was entitled "Money Mastery" and I thought it was about one thing — getting more. I found out that **true prosperity is giving more, not getting more**. He shared a formula with us for finding our purpose in life.

Answer the following questions. Be as honest as you possibly can, remember — no one is going to see this but yourself. Use extra paper if needed and really **express yourself**.

1. List 3 positive qualities about yourself (use adjectives). If it's difficult for your to narrow down three positive qualities about yourself, think about what people say about you.

_____

_____

_____

2. List 3 ways you enjoy expressing those qualities. (Use verbs or things that you enjoy doing.)

_____

_____

_____

3. If you were going to create an ideal world, what 3 adjectives would describe your ideal world?

_____

_____

_____

After deriving the answers to these 3 questions, combine your answers and create a paragraph like the following.

MY PURPOSE:

To utilize my ability to (#1) inspire, motivate and heal through (#2) writing, lecturing and singing. Everyone, including me, experiences (#3) unconditional love, abundance and freedom.

Complete the exercise and write the paragraph on about 5 index cards. Keep them visible. Good places to put them are bathroom, kitchen, the dash board in your car, on your desk, bedroom, or wherever you spend time automatically.

I know this assignment may seem like a very elementary one, and it is. Yet it is so powerful. Why? **Because what we focus on we give "power."** Clarity and focus will take you far quickly. I have heard it said **where the mind goes, the power flows.** What we focus on expands. As you focus on your purpose, opportunities will open up for you to express your purpose. God gave you your gifts and talents so that you would express them, and in expressing them you are expressing God. We are all here to bear witness to the awesomeness and the glory of God. All of us feel this desire for self-expression. Until we begin to express or share our gifts we experience frustration, unhappiness and depression.

Answer the following questions. Again, use more paper if you need.

ॐ

1. What are some things you believe you do well?

_____

_____

_____

_____

_____

2. *What are some things you think you are not very good at?*

_____

_____

_____

_____

_____

3. *If given the chance, I think I MIGHT be good at:*

_____

_____

_____

_____

_____

4. *One NEW thing I have tried recently and it went pretty well was:*

_____

_____

_____

_____

5. Who encouraged me to try #4? What made him/her think I could do that? Does she/he often encourage me to try a new thing?

_____

_____

_____

_____

_____

6. Who are the mentors (the wise, loyal advisers) in my life?

_____

_____

_____

_____

ॐ

Forget for a moment about making money. What is it that you'd do if you had all the money you could ever need or want? I have seen this principle work in the lives of many people. A woman said she loved baking cakes and she began to bake them. She put a great deal of love and creativity into the cakes. Through a series of divine events, she received a commercial oven and received contracts for her cakes in many exclusive shops and elegant restaurants.

Begin now doing the things you really enjoy doing. Start sharing what you enjoy with others and doors will open for you. **Faith without works is dead**.

In a book entitled *Creating Money* by Sanaya Roman & Duane Packer, there is an entire section on discovering your life's work. Often times we wonder why we are in certain positions or jobs. Every job, hobby and experience is important in the overall scheme of things. And of course, we don't understand now because we are incapable of seeing the entire picture. Hindsight is always 20/20. We are able later to see why we were in certain positions and we say, "Oh yea, ok, this is why I was working here learning this skill."

Remember that your yearning to be, to do and to have is Spirit seeking to express itself in you. When you really realize this it will become quite clear that there is unique work for you to do and this work is an established fact in the mind of God. God has already prepared for you that which is your very own. When an idea continues to nag you, tugs at your heart, and constantly wakes you up at 3:30 in the morning it is because God is trying to tell you something.

Listen. Open yourself to the awareness that there is a divine plan for your life and that it was knitted inside of you when you were in your Mother's womb. How do you get in touch with it? You must **pray and then listen**, listen to your heart. Sit in the silence and practice feeling and being open to The Presence. Then, **follow your heart**. As you continue to vision like this on a daily basis, your life's work will reveal itself in your mind and it will actually manifest.

State this affirmation for 21 days:

"I am now open and receptive to my purpose in life. I am willing to express the gifts and talents that the Creator has endowed me with. I now release from my thinking any ideas of limitation, lack or restriction. I listen to my heart, for it is connected to my soul. I accept my ideal work. I live my vision. I am fulfilled. And so it is."

When anyone asks me to do anything, I think about my purpose. Is this request in alignment with my purpose? If it is, I say yes and if it is not, I say "no." The Universe supports me when I operate my life by being on purpose. I always know when I am on purpose because of all the unconditional love, abundance and freedom that I experience.

Get clear about your purpose before you start seeking employment. Start with a clear focus and you will see how amazingly things will open up for you. Read your purpose and give thanks in advance for opportunities to do your purpose. You will begin to create a new groove in your mind.

Sara was out of work and she decided that she would share one of her many talents with a friend who operated a small business. She knew this friend really needed help and that she would not be able to pay her. But Sara had a need to get out of the house, to give and to keep busy. She gave first and as she was "in the flow," things began to happen. Her employer received a large contract within 10 days and Sara was given a small salary. Within 30 days an unexpected check came for several thousand dollars and she was offered a very well-paying position.

Don't wait for a traditional position! **Give, and the law says you will receive,** and you will receive a multiplied return. **As we give, we receive.** When we give freely, we receive freely.

One of my many positions was that of a Coordinator of a volunteer program. I have seen many people volunteer their time and then receive a permanent position. My mentor who held the same position at another organization said that *"Volunteers are the richest people in the world, because they are people who know they have something to give."* In this society we are always concentrating on getting, getting, and getting some more. This getting mentality is one of fear and belief in scarcity.

The yearning to be all that we can be is "Spirit" seeking to express itself in us. As we realize this, it becomes clear that there is unique work for each of us to experience and that this work has already been established in God's mind.

Your life's work will reveal itself to you — you don't have to try and rack your brain to figure it out. Focus on your purpose and look for ways to be about the business of your purpose and observe what just naturally develops. When you are on purpose the Universe will just send you money, opportunities and fulfillment.

Peggy was feeling like she was worthless one day and that she needed a platform from which to minister. That same day a young lady called her in distress. The doctors told her she had bone cancer and that her time on planet earth was very limited, perhaps 2 months. Peggy spent three hours ministering to her. She prayed with this lady and encouraged her. When Peggy hung up Spirit said to her, "You don't need a church, an office or a Ph.D, just minister to those I bring to you and I will supply all of your needs." The lady Peggy ministered to is still alive, and that was 10 years ago. Peggy is living a very prosperous life traveling, lecturing, looking great and staying on purpose.

Our task is to open ourselves to the awareness that there is a divine plan for this world and that we are a part of that divine plan. We may not know where we fit and we don't have to know, we need only trust, and <u>wait</u> for direction. **When there is a desire and willingness to serve capably and efficiently, there is also a position ready and waiting to be filled.** The supply is always equal to the demand.

Keep your mind stayed on the truth that **God is your source** and don't be afraid. Go forth secure in the knowledge that God is unerringly leading you into new avenues of service and worthwhile achievements.

Jan was unemployed and burned out. She told the Creator she needed three months of rest and she could trust that the Creator would provide a way that her bills would get paid. Money came from unexpected sources and she looked about 10 years younger after the three months had passed. She then decided to ask the Creator for an ideal position. She decided what type of office she'd like to be in. She liked an office that has very modern with modern furniture, plants, and windows with lots of sun peering through. She decided that she wanted to work with very progressive thinking people.

Jan was very clear that she needed flexibility; she wanted to work where she could be picking up skills that would benefit her in the future and she was clear that she wanted to travel. She visualized and prayed often. Bills were due and there were many days that she was quiet and desperate. She was hired as a trainer and she hated the classroom teaching environment. She fasted for 3 days and prayed and within 21 days she landed a position in the same organization at the Corporate Office. Her supervisor was very progressive, the office was modern with plants, windows and sun peering through. She had to travel in this new position and other amenities were added that she didn't ask for. The office was in the center of rich culture, beautiful shops, fantastic restaurants and very close to her home.

Get clear about your gifts. List 10 or more interests that you have, and make sure these interests are things that you enjoy doing. For each interest think about a time you did it and how it made you feel. Write all of this out because **writing crystallizes thought**. Read and reread your interests list and now write down the skills involved in each interest. This exercise will assist you in becoming clearer about your gifts and talents. Finally, make a determination of which skills you can utilize in a position or business. Remember, resumes tell only what type of work you have done. You make be skilled to do far greater things, so sell your skills.

Shelia visualized that she would work with a very progressive training organization and learn everything about the training industry since that was what she loved to do. She began training in the organization and found that she did not enjoy it. She felt so burned out at the end of the day. She immediately began visualizing herself writing the programs for other trainers and traveling for the company. In two weeks she was transferred to the Program Development Department and was traveling the United States to monitor the programs that were implemented.

How all is this is going to happen is not your business. The Lord will handle all the details for you. Your part is to see it and sense it. What you see is what you get.

Chapter VIII

HEALTH IS THE BIRTHRIGHT OF THE SPIRITUAL WOMAN

'Know ye not that ye are the temple of God?'
I Corinthians 3:16

Every 2 minutes 3 women die from breast cancer. Every 2 minutes 3 women are diagnosed with breast cancer. In one hour 90 women have died with breast cancer and 90 have been diagnosed. These statistics are astounding.

Breasts are symbols of nurturing. **There is an underlying spiritual connection to every disease**. Breast cancer is connected to lack of nurturing **self**. Women have to learn how to nurture themselves. They must learn how to get **balance** in their lives.

Breast cancer is the number one killer of African-American women. We have nurtured the world and we really must begin nurturing ourselves more. At this juncture it's imperative that we begin to love and nurture ourselves to be fit vessels to carry the healing to the nation. In Bell Hooks' book, *Sisters of the Yam* she says, "It is the absence of love that has made it so difficult for us to stay alive or, if alive to live fully."

God lives inside of you. 'Thou shall have no other God before me,' saith the Lord. If God is inside of you, you must honor yourself in order to please God. Your temple is the dwelling place of God. We can no longer get away with defiling the temple.

We are in a time of acceleration. Things are moving much too fast. **Stop running from your demons.** Unresolved issues quietly drain your energy. You may not be consciously aware that certain issues are unresolved. One way to become of aware of your issues is to check out the issues of those whom you have attracted in your life to be your friends, mates, and co-workers. We learn so much from our relationships with others; remember, **they are our mirrors**. As you deal with your own demons and feel whole, you will attract different type of people; people who are now where you will be at a future moment and time.

Stop trying to block off what hurts you. Feel your feelings and take them all to the Master. Expose your heart to God and ask for a miracle for each one of those hurts. In blocking off what hurts us, we think we are walling ourselves off from pain. But in the long run, the wall which prevents growth, hurts us more than the pain. If you'll hang in there for a moment with the pain, it will subside and be resolved. It's like when we get massages. The therapist may find a knot. If she/he works it out you are definitely in pain, yet as it is worked out, the muscle relaxes, the pain is gone and you gain more energy for your use. When we build walls of protection or defense, we simultaneously keep the good out too. It can make you feel so vulnerable to put your wall down, yet this is also an opportunity to practice trusting.

The Course in Miracles says, "My defenselessness is my defense." The battles aren't yours to fight. Stop fighting for or against things. **What we fight with, we bond with.** We often hear organizations have a slogan like, "Leading the fight against cancer." You don't want to fight with cancer;

you want to **be pro-active** and busy doing the things you need to do mentally, emotionally, physically, and politically to make a difference. I can't stand it when election time comes around and each candidate destroys the other with words. It is so immature and it's the sign of so very unenlightened people. Perot came along in a past election and **showed** them a different way. He refused to get caught up in the mudslinging, and this was refreshing.

As a **spiritual** women , a part of your wealth is that you have a partner — God or the Higher Power. This power will guide you in every decision.

Listen

Trust

and

Obey.

This requires practice. I have been asked often, "How do I know when it is God talking to me or whether it is just me?" Well, the scriptures say 'God's sheep know his voice.' God's sheep know his voice first of all because they are God's sheep, made out of God and they have developed a **relationship** with God. You know your Mother's voice because you have spent decades interacting with her. You will know God's voice as you interact with God. Remember that interaction is a two-way street. You pray and then you listen to what God has to say, which may be in the form of thoughts, visions, ideas or hearing in your own voice. In all thy ways acknowledge God first. Go to God first and you will always be successful.

I have counseled too many broken women who have given and given and given some more, but who don't receive. Many of them don't even know **how** to receive. They are busy from sun up to sun down "doing good." As

Rev. Cecilia Bryant put it, "They are doing good and still caught up in their eating disorders, doing good and hurting, doing good and never stopping long enough to heal themselves." Nurturer, it's time to nurture yourself. **Giving is receiving** and it is just as important to receive as it is to give because to give without receiving creates an incomplete circle.

Another problem that I have observed with many women is their inability to say no. We crave love so much, we think we need another's approval so much that we carry an overwhelming amount of guilt. The guilt and the lack of balance in our lives creates tremendous stress. **Stress is a response**. Our bodies are saying, "I have taken in too much. I have swallowed too many pain sentences, I have taken in too many sweets when what I was looking for was some sweetness in my life."

Thinking that you are in control is quite stressful too. **You are not in control.** You may think you are; however, you aren't. Be glad that you don't have to make any decisions alone. You are a child of God; you must act like a child in order to enter into the kingdom. That means trusting in God's way. God's way is not your way. Surrender your way for the way of success. God can only be a success.

M. Scott Peck in *The Road Less Traveled* says, "One of the roots of mental illness is invariably an interlocking system of lies we have been told and lies we have told ourselves." Lies do hurt! If we really want to be whole, healthy and happy we **must** voice our truth. Wearing the mask can be an activity that kills us. Pretending that everything is ok when it isn't and saying yes when your heart is clearly telling you no, is working against the grain. Healing starts when we begin to own how we really feel and when we are able to tell our truth being loving, open and honest.

72

Wellness can only come about when we are dedicated to truth.

Peck says, "People who are honest and open can feel free. They are not burdened by a need to hide. They do not have to slink around in the shadows. They do not have to contract new lies to hide old ones. They don't need to waste effort covering tracks or maintaining disguises." The truth does make us free.

Own all of your stuff. Spend time checking your stuff out. An unexamined life is not worth living.

Speak your truth without intentionally hurting someone else. You must look at your intent and motive. We find it easy to tell it like it is when we are enraged. That's the time **not** to talk. It is important that you not use truth to inflict pain on anyone. As you give, so you receive. And I want you to know what I know for sure — when stuff starts coming back in, it is definitely multiplied. Multiplied pain can make you wish you were dead. Remember you are **always** dealing with yourself. **We are one.**

I have taught many assertiveness training sessions and it is quite evident that we need to practice speaking our truth. We define a passive person as one who doesn't consider themselves and always considers the needs of others. An aggressive person considers their needs only and could care less about the needs of others. And an assertive person considers their own needs *and* the needs of others. Assertiveness is the goal of a wealthy spiritual woman.

We must take the time to define healthy limits in our lives. We haven't learned how to set protective boundaries that would eliminate certain forms of stress in our lives. Defining boundaries is linked to us honoring and valuing ourselves.

Society rewards us most when we are willing to push ourselves to the limit and beyond. We are most valuable when we do this. *Valuable to whom?* How can we resist this agenda? Take time to reassess your lifestyle. Put it on paper like slices of a pie. Is there time for cultural enrichment? Being creative? Exercise? Relationships? Spiritual needs? Look at how you spend your time and then look at how you would *like* to spend your time. **Awareness always precedes change**. Looking at it on paper always allows one to be more objective. Plan time for yourself. You owe it to God. Your body is the temple of God. God lives in there, so treat God good.

ક

Slice up the pie below, representing by size how much time you give to the following areas. If it helps, you can assign percentages or fractions.

_____ cultural enrichment   _____ creativity
_____ exercise   _____ relationships
_____ spiritual growth   _____ work

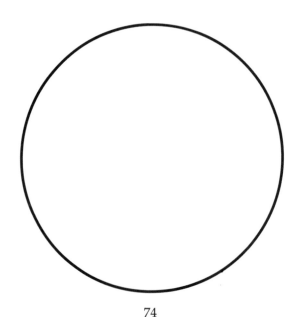

Now, draw a circle and design your pie with the emphasis on how you'd ideally like your life divided.

Did you realize that worry never solves anything? Actually it blocks solutions from coming to you. To worry is to fill your mind with negative thoughts. It is like praying, but you are praying negatively. When well-meaning relatives and loved ones tell me, "I worry about you when I don't hear from you," I respond, "please don't. Just **know** that wherever I am, God is." In Susan Jeffers' book, *Feel the Fear and Do It Anyway*, she says, "It is reported that over 90% of what we worry about never happens. That means that our negative worries have a 10% chance of being correct."

A friend of mine called me yesterday to tell me that the statistics on the longevity of women have changed. She said, "If we can bypass cancer and heart disease we can live to be 92." Wow, we can really do some living, exploring and learning! If we are living longer we must certainly want to live longer healthy.

Every day is filled with choices. This understanding of passive, aggressive and assertive behavior becomes vital when we are making choices. Whenever you make a choice it is important to consider how the choice is going to affect you and the other person and speak from that position. **Women have to practice saying no.** If you find this to be true about you, begin practicing today. Many superwomen are the women with strokes, heart attacks and other stress-related disorders.

God is everywhere and evenly present. Everything that exists or ever will exist is pressed out of the body of God. Woman is pressed out of the body of God. Woman is divine. The nature of a thing is its essential character. God's nature is absolute good. We are an idea in God's mind. We were made in God's image and likeness. **If God created you perfect, you are still perfect.** There is a part of you that is untouched by cancer, aids or tumors. You must understand the truth about you.

The truth is that you are a spiritual being and Spirit can't get sick. You live in a spiritual universe and in that realm there is no sickness. In order for healing to permeate and saturate your physical body you must be clear about this truth and enter that realm often and stay there for sufficient periods until the healing process is complete.

I met a lady who had been diagnosed with cancer. She had been receiving radiation treatments and she had gotten very weak. She began praying and meditating and during one of her meditations the Spirit of God spoke to her and told her that his radiation of Love would heal her if she would just continue to come in, to come ye from among them. She daily spent time within and feeling the love radiation from God and today she is whole.

Life is one of the main ideas or qualities of God. There is only one life and that life is your life now. In the idea of Life are involved all the potentialities of that which is evolved through woman. **Life is an idea in Divine Mind. Woman is an idea in Divine Mind. Life and woman co-exist.** As the daughter is to the mother so is the idea to the mind. Father (God-Mind) is one with its offspring, the idea — the son. The Father and Son are one — they are coexistent, there is continual interaction and communion. It was from the grand idea of Divine Life that Jesus healed the sick and raised the dead. The idea itself becomes the evolving power through which it makes itself manifest. We bring divine ideas into manifestation by making ourselves one with them, by becoming conscious of our indwelling Christ Mind and our oneness with the Father/Mother God.

Jesus always gave thanks in advance and became one with the power. Thus the power manifested through Jesus in a very mighty way. The perfect idea can produce only perfect results. For one who wants to have such results in her life, she must watch the thoughts in her mind. She needs to be certain to entertain only healthy, loving and positive thoughts because the law of manifestation for woman is the law of thought. **Every thought is a prayer.**

Health is our birthright; there is a fundamental principle of health pervading all forms. Health is not something that has to be manufactured from without; it is the very essence of Being, and is therefore enduring and universal as God is. It is our birthright, yet God has given us free will and so we must **choose** health. We must choose to claim our inheritance. In *Let Healing Through* by James Dillet Freeman he says, "Only God can make healing happen; only God heals." We think, say, or do things that let the healing force work; all healing comes from God.

Since God's nature is Absolute Good and Life is its nature and essential character, it is God's will that we have perfect health. We are God's offspring; it's our inheritance.

Webster says to inherit means "to come into possession of, as an heir, to receive by nature from progenitor." A progenitor is a forefather or a foremother. An heir is one who receives or is entitled to receive any endowment of quality from a parent predecessor. To be an heir of God means to be a daughter of God. To be an heir of God means to have attained a **consciousness** of true relationship with God. This idea of Life is at the mental command of God's heirs, yet many are unaware of what God's plan is for them and this world and that it is absolutely good. **It is essential that we get an understanding of who God is and who we are in God. We must claim our inheritance.**

An example was given in my intensive studies at the Johnnie Coleman Institute in Chicago, Illinois. "Someone has left you $250,000," the teacher said to the group. "What would you have to do to receive it?" After many thoughts and explanations, one of the students said, "You must show your identification card."

"Who are you?" Show your card and enter into The Absolute Good Redemption Center. What do they sell, you might ask? They sell nothing. Yet you will be given whatever it is that you think you stand in need of in the physical realm.

Where is this place? It is inside of you. Deep inside of your heart and soul. It's that place that you automatically go to when so called "devastating things" happen to you. You don't even try to go there then, God's great love and eternal compassion just shifts us there because we are rendered totally helpless.

I had a dear friend named once name Joy. Joy was bright, creative, loving, pretty and wise. She had about 4 children and she had been recently divorced. She called me one Tuesday afternoon and told me that she had just been diagnosed with cancer. She asked me to pray with her. We prayed and God touched her at that moment. Her mind was touched to make some decisions. To become active in her own healing process. The decisions that would come in the coming months were difficult and yet healing. Two of Joy's boys were over 17 and one was very disruptive. She made a decision for him to stay with a relative. "I will die if I don't create peace in my environment. I love my son but this boy has got to leave here or I will die." This is what **tough love** is all about.

We made a commitment to pray often and not to tell too many people about it. We learned early on the power of secrets with God. He says 'if you will go into your secret closet, I will reward you **openly.**'

Joy made the decision to stop working because her job was too stressful. She decided she wouldn't drive for awhile because she needed to feel as if she was being chauffeured (an act of nurturing herself). So she took cabs everywhere. Joy also got her telephone turned off, and journaled. The work she needed came to her. She went to radiation and of course they told her of all their limiting beliefs that her hair would fall out, that she would lose weight and she would feel sick.

"No I won't," she insisted. "I will not lose my hair, I will not lose weight and I will not feel sick after this radiation treatment because **God is in these rays and God is with me.** I am healed in the name and the nature of Jesus Christ." Well the doctor looked in amazement and she had several treatments in the following 3 months. Her hair grew, she gained weight and her cancer went into remission.

Joy followed a wholistic program for the treatment of her condition. Her diet consisted of brown rice, steamed vegetables, carrot juice, herbal teas, 8 to 10 glasses of distilled water a day, fresh fruit. She included colonics, extra rest, prayer, and meditation (God's radiation table). **This program of natural health care did what medical science alone could not.**

We must return to eating from the earth. The sun transfers the healing life force into the plants, fruits, grains and herbs. Embrace the life force. Don't make it hard, **just be willing to make a change** and the Creator will help you to make that change.

There is a correlation between the struggles that women face and the ecological movements that seek to restore balance to the planet . It was almost unbelievable to me when I saw how the government wanted to start legislation regulating the use of herbs. Diseases and dependencies are profitable. Yet by the Grace of God, more and more people are taking their health into their own hands by eating right, exercising, thinking right and serving God.

Seek out support. Share with one another ways to process pain and grief. Susan Jeffers in *Feel The Fear and Do It Anyway* says, "Acknowledgment of pain is very important; denial is deadly. Pain can be incredibly destructive if kept submerged.. Unacknowledged pain is subtly destroying many people's lives." Unacknowledged pain eats away at our health. Being healthy is our birthright— claim your inheritance!

Chapter IX

SPIRITUAL PARENTING

'Believe on the Lord and thou shalt be saved and thy house.' Acts 16:31

Most homes are headed by a single woman. The spiritual woman understands however, that her children are not her children; her children have a **heavenly** mother and father. Kahlil Gibran says, "Your children are not your children, they are children of Life's longing for itself."

When my daughter turned 14, I felt that I should stop facilitating parenting workshops. I felt so hopeless and had no solutions. Oh, how we grow when we are in the valley! This challenging experience was one of growth for me as much as it was for her.

My daughter began to express very openly all of my fears. I had no control over her and I literally left my job 3 or 4 times a week for some problem at school or trying to find out where she was when she skipped school. I was moving through a divorce at this time and everything seemed so out of control and frightening. I prayed a lot and one night I went to the river to pray with my significant other. When we are walking back to the car a woman approached me and said, "I know your heart is heavy. God wants me to tell you that it's going to be alright, your daughter is going to be alright and one day she will come to you and ask your forgiveness for these difficult experiences." God uses people and we never know when we are entertaining angels.

During this period, I felt so weak, tired and strained. I was trying to make a decision if it wouldn't be better for her to be with her Father. Because of my questions and thoughts, of course, I attracted friends and relatives who questioned me. They were mirroring my fears. "How are you going to let her live with her father at such a vulnerable age?" "What about all those gangs in Los Angeles?" Every question I asked myself silently, they asked me audibly.

I let her go to live with her Father. It was painful but I did it and it was the best thing that I could have done. One of my best friends moved to Los Angeles shortly after my daughter moved there and she spent quality time with her. Two other women in her Father's complex spent quality time with her and she got insights about me, herself, family and the world that I could never have given her. Just as the woman at the water had predicted, she did come back and ask for forgiveness.

I'd like to share with you the spiritual treatment, the spiritual affirmation or prayer that I used:

"I speak this word for my daughter remembering that she is God's child, and my own chief duty is to love her. I have been so caught up in the appearance of her problems that I have forgotten who she really is. This young person has an immortal soul and is a Divine being. I bless my child to an awakening of her real identity. God in me now salutes God in her.
"For he shall give his angels charge over her, to keep her in all thy ways." Psalm 91:11.

After the beating death of a young man in our city, his priest said, "The problem was not the youth, but the parents." Dr. Thomas Hora, psychologist and author of *Beyond the Dream,* said, "Children reflect the consciousness of their parents or parental figure." This means that the behavior of our children is usually an indication of some cleaning up that we need to do in our own consciousness as parents. **We are not talking about blame here, only** *awareness*.

We program our children even as they are in our womb with our attitudes, beliefs, thoughts, and circumstances surrounding the pregnancy. Until we deal with our own consciousness, all of our attempts to "fix" a child are only going to compound the situation. As problems arise, ask yourself, "What is the message this challenge is telling me about myself?" What am I learning from all of this? What do I need to learn from all of this?

My work experience includes me serving as a counselor for family and teen programs. When talking to parents they invariably talk about how impossible the child is. Their focus is usually on the child. What's wrong with the child? How can we change or fix the child? Rarely was there one who wanted to look at her or himself and say, "How can I change, grow or become a better parent for this child? How have I contributed to this situation?"

Our relationships are always mirrors reflecting back to us some aspect of ourselves. We homo sapiens have a tendency to want to change or fix something or someone outside of ourselves as the source of our difficulty. It is important to realize that we cannot change anyone or make anyone fulfill our unrealized dreams, shattered hopes or unfulfilled aspirations.

Children mirror parents and this is quite frightening to parents. Kids act out our fears. Stop fearing and start loving. There are only two emotions in the world: fear and love, and you can't fear and love simultaneously. Both emotions are very powerful and both are magnetic. **We get what we fear**. Children are born capable and are teachers and students.

Kate, a 40-year old single parent, states, "My daughter got pregnant. That was my greatest fear for her other than her physical safety. Now that this has happened, I can relax because my greatest fear has already happened."

Our thoughts and feelings create our experience and yes, it's hard work to keep vigilance over our thoughts and feelings. Our words are powerful and it's work to keep vigilance over our words too. We say, "You're wet, you are going to catch a cold." The child accepts this statement and it moves into the subconscious mind, and before night falls or the sun rises they are sniffing and hacking. We say, "You are just like your mother or father, they are so and so and so are you." This feeds the mind and thus creates the candidates for jails, half-way houses and recovery centers.

When you have had a bad day at work and you are irritable, kids pick up on that energy and they become cranky too. The next time havoc is being wrecked in your home, try this experiment. Go to your room and become very quiet. See if this doesn't change the energy of the rest of your household.

You really need a spiritual life when you are raising a family. We need to meditate and pray often to establish that spiritual relationship with the Creator. As we establish that relationship we get all the love, support and acceptance that we have sought all of our lives.

Let us pray to be open, receptive, loving, nurturing, supportive, and accepting. Let us pray that our children are open and receptive to the revealing of Spirit to them.

My quest for wholeness accelerated as I began to realize that I needed wholeness in order to transfer wholeness into my children's lives. As I began to accept my daughter unconditionally, I began to take my blinders off and see how she would act out my own unresolved issues. The apple really doesn't fall far from the tree. When you are busy hiding or denying your unresolved issues, you find that it really isn't hidden at all. It comes rushing out in the lives of our children.

Find a friend you can trust and one who doesn't feel she or he has to give you advice or judge. This friend ideally would be a good listener. Be honest with yourself. Feel your feelings — they are yours, all of them are yours. Surrender all to God and ask for help. Ask for guidance and inspiration.

No one can argue with your feelings. When people say to you, "Oh, but you shouldn't feel like that." Your response can be, "Don't should on me, love, this is the way I feel." **Stop judging yourself and don't give others permission to judge you**. Feel your feelings and express your feelings. Give yourself permission to look at what's happening in your family. Don't blame yourself, just become aware and know that **awareness is the first step to change**.

Parent, heal thyself! The nurturer needs nurturing. It is imperative that you nurture yourself. Make it a goal. Put some "me time" in your date book. Plan it in your schedule and make it a priority, one of those appointments you dare not cancel. Nurture yourself and let this be the beginning of the process of healing for your entire family. When you are taking care of yourself, you do the greatest service to others.

If you are one of those "smothering" mothers, consider that sometimes excessive caretaking doesn't allow our children to grow. They become dependent, weakened and crippled. Animals seem to be more intelligent than we so called "humans" in this area. Many species push their young out into the experience of life when they are very, very young. I've seen too many people who have been crippled by parents. Some of them have never left home. Some of them have left home, yet the parents are still controlling them and some are even married and the parents control the marriage. Some of them have been tied into the parent through "guilt." **Don't do guilt**, it kills. Making your children feel guilty is definitely a "control" mechanism. Resist the temptation!

Remember that children are more capable than you think they are. The same God that made you, also made them. God has no grandchildren; they are God's children too. Kahlil Gibran says, "Your children are not your children, they are sons and daughters of life's longing for itself." They are not here for us to make them into what we want them to be. Spirit has a plan for their lives and their inner soul will reveal to them **in due time** what course they should take. Spirit does not need us to tell **its** children what to do. We are here to love them. If we do that, the Creator of them and us will take care of the rest. Now do you believe that? Do you trust God with your children? Is Allstate safer to us than God?

I have counseled with many people who are still struggling with getting their parents' approval. They are heavy-laden with guilt because they didn't fulfill their parents' fantasy of what they had in mind for their lives. Many parents have unrealized dreams and they want to realize those dreams through their children. More often than not, the parent doesn't even realize that this is what is occurring. Many people have shattered hopes and unfulfilled aspirations. Since they feel the connection with their offspring they begin to subconsciously send that message to the child and begin to unconsciously attempt to shape their children into a form that will provide fulfillment for themselves.

I cringe when I hear people say that we have a "Lost Generation." Words have so much power and so I always cancel it in my mind when I hear it. This so-called "Lost Generation" saw the president of the United States get caught in lies and deceit. This same "Lost Generation" has watched the high authorities of religion who people think are closer to God than others, be indicted for molestations whose number are growing so rapidly that it makes your head swim. Their parents are caught up in the endless treadmill of Corporate America where the only power is the almighty dollar at any cost. Listen to some of the lyrics of some the rap they listen to and they are telling you that they are not stupid and they are angry.

Stop blaming the children, stop blaming the parents and stop blaming society and racism. Yes it exists and I say, so what. We are spiritual beings, we live in a spiritual realm and as spiritual beings we know we cannot solve problems at the level of the problem; we have to come up and little higher. **We are not victims, we are more than overcomers**, we have power, authority and dominion. We are Davidas (as in David and Goliath), and we have that same stone that slayed the so-called Giant.

I had the privilege of working with a group of teens and parents in a program entitled, "Choose To Live." One day I asked the teens if they could tell their parents one thing that they felt would improve their relationship, what would that one thing be? Ninety per cent said, "I would tell them to **listen**." Being a parent, I know it is sometimes difficult to **just listen** without putting in our two cents. They want us to listen with our hearts and our **undivided** attention. Sometimes we are cooking, typing or cleaning and we are listening while we are working. Well that's not good enough, they deserve your undivided attention. Give your child at least 5 minutes of undivided attention and listen to them. Practice listening without judging and without thinking about what you are going to say next while they are talking. Just listen.

On the following pages are some guidelines and tips that can help guide you to a more spiritual approach to parenting. Write them down, tear them out or copy them and hang them on your wall. Refer mentally to them when you are in a conversation with your child or dealing with a problem with them. Just as our children must practice the skills necessary to become responsible adults, so we must practice our parenting skills in order to give our children the best of our experience.

ह

GUIDELINES FOR SUCCESSFUL SINGLE PARENTING

1. Don't try to be both parents to your children.

2. Don't force your children into playing the role of the departed parent.

3. Be the parent you are. Don't abdicate your parent position for that of a big brother, big sister, or a buddy.

4. Be honest with your children. Tell them the truth about what you are feeling.

5. Assist them in owning their feelings and open your heart; let them express themselves without your judgment. Our feelings are just that — our feelings, and they really can't be argued with; at most, they can be understood.

6. Don't make your children or grandchildren undercover agents who report on the parent's current activities.

7. Children who have experienced divorce still need both parents. Don't deny their right to experience the other parent because of your own personal feelings, i.e. revenge, anger, and resentment.

8. Share your dating life and social interest with your children.

9. Help your children keep the good memories of the past marriage alive. Don't rob the children of their happy memories.

TIPS FOR EFFECTIVE PARENTING

1. Effective parenting requires that the nurturer gets nurtured. What do you do to nurture yourself? Wilma Rudolph said, "The most important part of good health and relief of stress is surrounding yourself with people who love you." The people who love you are not *always* your family. They are not always some of the folk you call "friends." You know when you are in the presence of people who really love you. We haven't been taught to reach out for support. It seems it's a sign of weakness. We always want to appear that we've got it all together.... we've got it going on. Then one day we have a nervous breakdown or heart attack and everyone is so shocked. Seeking support is the sign of a mature and wise woman. Consciously surround yourself with "supportive" friends who are loving, kind and nurturing. Some friends are negative and they speak negatively in a joking manner. It doesn't matter that it's disguised in a joking manner; it's negative and you can't afford their company.

2. Children are born capable. Children are learning and teaching. What have you learned from a child lately?

3. When punishing a child it is very important **not** to attack their personhood. Express disapproval of the act, **don't attack the individual.**

4. Wisdom is innate. No one can learn to be wise. Wisdom isn't necessarily something that comes with age.

5. Constantly nurture a child's self-esteem. Praise them more than blame them. It only takes a few seconds to praise your children. What we criticize withers and what we praise grows, blossoms and shines.

6. **Don't deny their feelings.** Their feelings are important. Assist them in getting in touch with their feelings. And say such things as "that must have hurt you, that must have disappointed you, that must have upset you." Too many people grow into their 40's and 50's so out of touch with their true feelings because they never got permission from their caregivers to feel and express their true feelings.

7. Children will naturally **rise** to the level of their caregivers' expectations.

8. Kids mimic parents and others. They "mirror" adults.

9. Being dishonest with children is so confusing to children that it is criminal. They **know** the truth on a deeper level and they are more in tune with that deep level because they are more recently disconnected from the "the deep" — the deep mystery of birth.

10. Children act out because they are really crying for love and attention.

11. Children can and must be taught to express their anger in appropriate ways.

12. It is damaging when one parent talks negatively about the other parent. Both parents are part of the child and the negative expression affects the child unconsciously.

Chapter X

PROSPERITY IS A STATE OF MIND

.'..it is God who giveth us richly all things to enjoy.'
I Timothy 6:17

It's very difficult to think and feel prosperity when the appearance of lack and limitation has swallowed you up and seemingly spit you out. Yet, until a change of mind occurs, the state of mind that produced your present circumstances will continue to reproduce your misery.

Abundance is the natural state of being. It is unnatural to be in lack. It means that we are not in alignment with the universe, for in all of nature the only thing that we see is abundance. Think for a moment about the abundance demonstrated in nature, the flowers, the trees, the vegetables, the bodies of water, the stars, stones, fish, etc. The various erroneous programs that we have eaten, digested and re-digested have us out of alignment. Not feeling our feelings has us out of alignment. Not allowing our consciousness to think in an unlimited way keeps us out of alignment.

All of our thoughts are creative, all of them. **Thinking prosperous thoughts brings prosperity**. As a woman thinketh, so is she. Speaking words of prosperity bring forth prosperity. Is that too simple? Well, the powerful transforming truths are very simple.

This is an excerpt from a letter I received from one of my workshop participants.

"I've been broke. I came from riches to rags. I felt guilty about my riches. I didn't enjoy my prosperity. I felt other people envied me or they wanted something from me that I wasn't willing to give. I began saying this money doesn't mean a d—n thing to me. I literally directed money to leave my world and it did. I had talked myself into believing I didn't deserve good anymore and those very beliefs manifested."

Be careful with your words and examine what you really believe about prosperity. How did your parents handle money? What messages did you pick up as a child? Was there lack at home? Do you believe that rich people are evil? Do you verbally announce that you don't really care about money yet inwardly you really like to have money?

Prosperity is more than money. Prosperity is good vibrant health, peace of mind, happy relationships and family life, divine work that you love, self-expression and more. Prosperity means different things to different people. What does it mean to you? (Think about it for a moment)

What's your ideal life like? What will money give you that you don't have right now? What deeper needs would money satisfy? Would having lots of money give you more security, freedom, a simpler lifestyle? Would having lots of money solve all of your problems?

From *Creating Money* by Sanaya Roman and Duane Packer: "You can start satisfying those needs right now. You can have a joyful, fulfilling life and realize your greater potential with the material things you want to create. The essence of anything that will serve your higher good is within your reach. The Universe doesn't say you can have what is good for you only after you have a million dollars.

The Universe says that whatever is for your higher good you can have right now, today.

Ask yourself what you want money to give you and then think of ways you can have the **essence** of those things right now. Some people might feel that money will make their life more simple. You can begin designing a simpler life now without the money by developing such qualities as inner peace and becoming more organized in your life. Whatever we feel money is going to bring, we can begin to **feel** those qualities within ourselves right now. As we radiate those qualities within we will draw all good into our lives.

Remember that all of your thoughts are creative. As you think, the very substance of the Universe creates a set of circumstances to bring forth into your experience those thoughts and feelings. Thinking and feeling go hand and hand. Thinking is a masculine faculty and feeling is a feminine faculty. When you integrate your thinking and feeling you have a marriage that will produce many children (ideas).

The first law of prosperity is order. Take time to get every area of your life in order — your home, car, and office. Give away clothes and other things you are not using. If you haven't worn it or used it in a year, you probably won't, so release it. This is called creating a vacuum. Nature abhors a vacuum and will send something to fill in the empty space. Clean out your garage, your junk room, your garage, and all those junk drawers. This outer activity will send a message to your subconscious mind that you are now into the "preparation" stage. You are preparing to receive your good. Make a list of everything and everyone you are grateful for. Gratitude and praise opens the doors of prosperity. **Practice seeing in your mind's eye the ideal**

life for yourself. As you flood your mind with these pictures, your subconscious mind will work for you 24 hours a day to bring this ideal into a physical form. Realize now that there are two worlds — one world with money and a second world without money. **It's the world without money (the kingdom within) that creates the world with money**. Take time daily to practice seeing the ideal high quality life. Everyone is not capable of seeing. If you are one of those people, practice sensing or feeling the abundant feeling, the peace, joy and comfort that prosperity brings. The state of mind is the key to the manifestation of the outer reality.

We have been taught to do and then you will have and by having you will be...as in "be somebody." Universal truth teaches you that you must BE first. You are right now all that you'll ever be. As you continue to realize that you start from success, you will automatically do those things that will allow you to have. Got it? BE first, then DO, and you will HAVE. Seek you first the kingdom of God and its righteousness. Go within and think the right thoughts and everything will be added unto you.

All good — no matter who it comes through — comes from One Source. ONE. Our good comes forth through many channels and the channels change from time to time, yet the Source never changes. Your Source is not your job, ADC, SSI, your mate or your business. **God is your Source and God is your supply**. God becomes the thing itself. *Get to that one*. **God is absolute good**, that is the very nature of God. **God is substance**. Substance is that invisible stuff that everybody and everything is made out of. Hebrews says, "Faith is the substance of things hoped for, the **evidence of things that are not seen**." Substance is God. Therefore, everyone and everything is made out of God. We live in the mind of God. We live, move and have our being in God.

When we think we are desiring something good, it is actually God presenting to us his idea of what he'd like to "sire" or father through us. All that we must be is willing to be an open vessel for God to bring these desires into manifest form. **Can you say yes to your dreams and desires?** Then say it. Yes! Bring it forth through me God, I am willing.

What type of relationship do you have with the Source? It's the nature of your relationship with the Source that creates your particular physical world. How do your perceive the Source? Is your Source loving and all-providing or is it a withholding and punishing Source? The Source is always affluent, abundant, whose very essence is Love !

People find it difficult to believe that it is necessary to give first if they are to receive. As you give, so shall you receive, means the spirit in which you give determines the manner in which you receive. Many feel they don't have enough to give. **If you are in need, you need to give fearlessly**. Money, time, and energy are interchangeable. If you don't have money, give your time, talents, your love and your energy.

Prosperity is the out-picturing of substance in our affairs. Substance is present everywhere. Some people call it the ethers. Substance is passive. **You must act on it.** It is up to you to shape it and mold it with your thoughts and feelings. We are shaping and molding it all the time whether we are aware of it or not. We can greatly influence our environment through mental treatments. There is such a thing as demonstrating a control of conditions. As we are successful in looking away from present conditions and accepting better ones, we prove that we have the ability to manifest.

Manifestation is a process of bring your ideas, concepts, visions and dreams from your inner world into your outer world where you experience them with your physical senses. As you think, you think into Divine Mind, setting a law into motion, which is creative and which contains within itself limitless possibilities. We can demonstrate at the level of our ability to know; beyond this, we cannot go. Divine mind only knows about us what we know about ourselves. The real work must be done in the interior of our minds. **Change is an inside job.**

As we take time each and every day to see our lives as we wish them to be and make a mental picture of our ideal, we are passing this picture over to the law. After we have completed this part of the process we can go about our business with a calm assurance that in the inner side of life something is taking place. When you begin to feel a sense of hurry or worry, begin to talk to yourself, "I know and give thanks that Divine Mind has already taken care of this."

What the law does for us, it must do through us. When there is no longer anything in our mentality which denies our word, a demonstration will be made; nothing can stop it. The law is Absolute. Remain receptive, positive and develop faith in the evidence of things not seen with the physical eye but which are eternal in the heavens. It is a law that the person who sees what they want to see, regardless of what appears, will someday experience in the outer what has so **faithfully** been seen within.

Prosperity Affirmations

1. The more I give, the more I receive and this is the law.

2. **I deserve to be prosperous.**

3. I am prosperity, I am made out of the exact same stuff that God is made out of.

4. **The only limits are the ones I place on myself.**

5. God receives pleasure prospering me. For it is said that *it is the Father's good pleasure to give me the Kingdom.*

6. Prosperity allows me to bless and prosper others.

7. **I am willing to receive all that Father-Mother God has for me.**

8. Money flows to me easily, abundantly, and immediately.

9. I use money wisely.

10. **My supply is unlimited and unfailing,** because God is unlimited and God never fails.

11. I am a member of the Royal Priesthood and yes, **I dare to prosper.**

12. I bless my creditors and debtors and money flows in magnetically.

13. Supply is always equal to the demand, this is law.

14. The Lord (law) is my shepherd, I am guided to my good.

15. I am God's daughter and I **shall not want !**

PROSPERITY'S COMMANDMENTS

1. I LOOK ONLY TO GOD FOR MY PROSPERITY.

2. I MAKE NO MENTAL IMAGES OF LACK.

3. I SPEAK NO WORD OF LIMITATION.

4. I LET GO AND LET GOD WORK IN MY AFFAIRS.

5. I DEAL HONORABLY WITH GOD AND
ALL HIS PAYCLERKS.

6. I KEEP MY WEALTH CIRCULATING WISELY.

7. I USE MY WEALTH FOR GOOD PURPOSES ONLY.

8. I NEVER STRIVE TO GET SOMETHING
FOR NOTHING.

9. I NEVER TALK POVERTY. I TELL THE TRUTH
ABOUT GOD'S ABUNDANCE.

10. I TAKE MY EYE OFF MY NEIGHBOR'S WEALTH.
I CLAIM MY OWN.

Chapter XI

WHEN IT'S TIME TO MOVE ON... DIVORCE

"To everything there is a season..." *(Ecclesiastes 3:1)*

Change isn't easy. We fear the unknown. We get comfortable; even if it's a miserable existence, it's known and we get comfortable even with misery. When we get real uncomfortable we talk, cry, complain and then we do something about it. We know one day, that this is the day to make a decision. How do you know the time is right to move on? You no longer need to talk to anyone about it anymore. You become quiet and you go into action. You refuse to listen to anybody's opinion. It becomes a matter of — am I living or am I dying?

Many people believe marriages are forever, and some are. When you go before the preacher and the preacher says, "What God has joined together let no man put asunder," It doesn't mean you're going to stay together and it doesn't mean God has joined you together. The preacher is not God; what **God** joins together, nobody can separate! Sometimes you are engaged in a very beautiful sacred ceremony, yet you may be participating in this ceremony with the wrong woman or man. We go though the ceremony sometimes in our hearts knowing it is not going to work but we're so needy and dependent we want to be with **somebody**— "just don't let me be lonely."

And yet we find the worst loneliness is the loneliness of being **with** a person and still feeling alone. Our emotional needs may not be being met yet we stay because we believe its a **sin** to leave. We don't want to be another statistic. "Everybody's getting a divorce. What are my parents going to say? What are the neighbors going to think? How are people going to view me? Will women think that I am after their husbands? What will I do about money? I can't make it without his money!" These questions bombard your mind.

The following are comments I have heard from counselees during my years of counseling:

"I don't remember the last time we've kissed; we have been in the same house and haven't slept together for 6 years but I'm going to wait on the Lord... He's an alcoholic and my life is miserable but he needs me... I'm staying until my last child graduates from High School."

So when do we know it's time to move on? We're all uniquely different, yet we're one. There's no patent answer. For some, it was time 10 years ago and you didn't so you suppressed all the anger, resentment, pain, and isolation and nurtured cancer, tumors, and other diseases.

Some choose to physically die in the relationship because they've been mentally and emotionally dead for so long anyway. I do not believe it is God's will that any man or woman stay in an abusive situation and I believe if you surrender — I mean really surrender — that you will know exactly when it is time to move on and move on **deliberately** with faith.

Sometimes God gives us 5 signs and we say, just give me one more sign... And that's ok because God is so loving, kind, and so very patient that you can get 50 signs if you need that. Relationships are over long before the Divorce comes. Divorce is so traumatic because it's like a death. We go through all of the stages that a bereaved person goes through when a loved one dies:

1. Shock   2. Denial   3. Anger
           4. Confusion   5. Acceptance

Some say divorce is worse than death because the person is still alive. When a relationship ends because of death there is no going back. If you are in the process of moving on, know that healing doesn't happen overnight. You may go through tremendous guilt — "it's all my fault." **It is never one person's fault**. Two people are in a relationship and both contribute to whatever the relationship is.

Don't allow well-meaning others to get involved. They weren't there, they didn't sleep with the two of you and they have no right to infringe. Whether they do or not depends on you.

Don't talk negatively about your mate to others — you're really talking about a part of yourself. You consciously or unconsciously contributed to whatever happened, and all of it is a learning process.

If you ever needed to pray, **pray now**. Pray around the clock, pray for yourself, family and your mate. See each other as two wounded veterans bandaged from head to toe. How would you treat a person bandaged from head to toe? Very carefully and very gently, I believe. No matter how strong the person may appear, they are hurting. Digs and arguments only add to the injury. Quietly do what you have to do. Maybe you'll have one or two real friends who'll be there to support you. Be selective and prayerful about the people you allow to be in your space at this time.

Examine what you are believing about your future. If you **see** yourself going to the poor house, you will. If you see the divorce being nasty and ugly, it will be. After years of prayer and fasting, one day I knew it was over. I had a zillion signs. I was in denial. We are in denial because we wanted to do what was **"right."** Yet I remembered I didn't ask God for a husband, I chose him. After 18 years and all types of illnesses all stemming from unhappiness, I finally faced the dance of divorce.

God worked with me. God showed me how to be loving during the process. We did not allow others to express their opinions We cut them off immediately. This was **our** marriage and that was **our** divorce. God helped us to decide what we wanted to do with property, children and assets and gave us the wisdom to use one lawyer. The lawyer was so amazed at our caring and cooperation, he didn't charge us a dime. The judge was amazed too and she questioned a few times about whether we were sure that this was what we really wanted to do. We were able to break bread together after the divorce and we are friends today

If I say "don't be afraid," I already know you will be anyway. Keep remembering that you are not alone. God is with you in all things. Acknowledge the Lord and he will direct your path, even in a divorce.

If you need to physically move, God will guide you to your perfect abode. Don't accept that you'll have less money. God is the source of every dime you have every spend. **God is the Source**. Not your job, your wife, your husband, not SSI, ADC or anybody but God. God will be there in those late nights talking to you, reassuring you and protecting you.

I assured my ex that he wasn't a failure because we were divorced and God assured me that I wasn't a failure. Our marriage wasn't a failure either, it was just time for us to walk on paths that we could not walk on together.

God has a sense of humor. Remember that, especially when you are those tight, uncomfortable, looks-like-devastation spots. Keep saying over and over "God has a sense of humor!" That's what I kept saying to myself while watching my estranged husband on national TV kissing another woman. "OK I know it's just a film, but we just separated 2 months ago and now the whole country is watching him kissing her." I dialogue with myself, "Yes I can see the hurt in his eyes and I can feel his pain." Yes I didn't want him to pursue acting but he didn't marry me as a minister either. Lord knows you can't know what's in a person's heart and soul. Sometimes paths split and you walk separate paths yet you are still on the same highway. You part physically yet there's so many ties mentally, spiritually, and emotionally.

We never wanted a divorce. We really didn't. We loved each other but we couldn't live together as husband and wife any longer because it was killing us. I had so many illnesses, I was so depressed that a sad mask had crystallized on my countenance. Pictures don't lie, do they?. Go back through your old pictures and your face tells the story. It tells you right where you were mentally and emotionally. Try it!

After so many trips to the doctor and hospital and some truthing sessions with God, myself and a few trusted souls I realized I had to get out. Now I know what so many well-meaning Christian sisters and brothers would say, "You needed more faith, you **should** have done this and that," so let me say this for the record — I did. I did everything, fasting, praying, praying with the elders, the saints, and counseling for 10 years and finally I got real clear that we had to move on. One night I literally saw an exit sign in my bed room and it was in a neon color. That's why I say, "God has a sense of humor." I rubbed my eyes thinking that I was dreaming and there it was. I ignored that sign because I wasn't ready.

After watching that first episode of "HEARTSPACE" — this is the name of series John was acting in — I did some heavy duty processing. I cried, I cried until I reverted back to crying as a child, feeling lonely and helpless. I was a miserable child but I had to allow myself to look at this thing in depth. "Lord change me at depth." That's part of the Master Mind Prayer that I repeat every week. So that's why I say, God has a sense of humor, because 'change me at depth' means you gotta go through something in depth, in other words, " deep."

I was happy that he had this part. He literally went to Hollywood with nothing but FAITH. That's why I say "God has a sense of humor," because John said to me one day, "You're always telling people, do what you really love to do and you'll be successful. Well acting is what I love and I have FAITH and that's all I need." It's an accelerated growth moment when those words come right back to you. You begin to understand that the **truth is a two-edged sword; it cuts and heals all at the same time.**

He stayed with one of my best friends when he went. That's why I say that God has a sense of humor. How comfortable was I with this? Some days very, some days not, some day not caring.

He was broken and I was broken. During my prayer time the Lord had shown me a vision of the two of us; we were bandaged from head to toe. What's does this mean, Father? "It means you two have wounded each other enough, as you move through this process, be gentle with each other." I shared this revelation with John and he accepted.

We decided to stop sleeping together and to remain in

the home to parent our two children who were ages 15 and 12. We maintained that existence for 3 years and I had gotten very tired of the existence because it was still strained somewhat, even though we were gentle with each other. One day John said, "I'm going to California to live in 2 weeks." God has a sense of humor because I was not employed at the time and neither was he. I had prayed for "divine resolution" and the day had come and I was filled with terror, emotion and rage.

Two days after his announcement, I spoke to a group of young girls in the basement of a community college about positive attitudes and conflict resolution. I told you, God had a sense of humor. As I was clearing out the candy wrappers from the floor a gentlemen walked into the room and asked me if I had a college degree. "Yes," I replied. "Well," he continued, "this college is looking for teachers right now. You don't need a teaching certificate, just a college degree." "Really!" God had opened up a way for me to survive, because that pay was only survival pay. Well, the rest is history, I taught there and provided for the basics to see me through to the next miracle that God would perform.

John was invited to a party two weeks after arriving in California. He said he really didn't feel like socializing but he talked himself into going. He met a well-know actress there who would in turn introduce him to an agent, a good agent as a matter of fact. You can't get work in Los Angeles without an agent. John sold himself and the agent began providing auditions immediately. John landed the part on "HeartSpace." I was happy for him and I was actually surprised at my reaction to viewing the series. The next two weeks were worst. They went from kissing to lovemaking to having a baby, all within 6 weeks. That's television for you.

Thank God for skilled, spiritual counselors who would

assist me in moving out of my pit to level ground again. God sent me the perfect counselor. She lived in Illinois, so she counseled me by telephone. She **knew** God for herself and that made all the difference. I knew that she was authentic and that she really cared about me — she did not even charge a fee. She was not clock watching as so many traditional therapists do. She allowed herself to be used by God and she took whatever time it took to see me through. God has a sense of humor and I eventually was able to **find** the humor. I eventually moved into a space of being grateful that my stuff was being played out on an actual TV screen so that I would really be impacted, so that I'd be forced to deal with myself, my STUFF!

My daughter began acting like someone possessed. I was wondering if someone had screwed her head off and put it back on improperly or something. It was like I was living with "the enemy." She began talking back, skipping school and lying. I had to leave work at least 3 times a week to go to her school for something. She was disrespectful to teachers, to me and to herself. She got involved with a young man and things really got totally out of control. I was torn, worn, and scorned. I had to take it to Jesus and leave it there for I had gotten to the point that there was nothing else that I could do.

One night I asked her to wash dishes and she said that she didn't feel like washing the dishes and that I better not touch her. Well my grandmom's spirit rose up in me and my great grandmother, the one I never met, and I was ready to "take her out of the world" as the old folk would say — "I brought you here and I will take you out of here!" I understood what that really meant. "I'm not going to hit you," I replied, "I'm going to kill you." My grandmother's spirit came out in me. My daughter reacted to my rage and hit me.

All I could see after that was death, somebody's. I stopped and called my former husband to come and get her right then and there 3,000 miles away. I wanted him there in 5 minutes because I wasn't going to be responsible for whatever else I was going to do and what was so scary is that I didn't know exactly what that was going to be. My former mother-in-law said someone was coming to get her about 10 minutes later and she proceeded to tell me how the impact of the divorce was probably affecting my daughter. I was beyond hearing anyone's words and I softly told her that "nothing justifies a child hitting a parent, just come and get her."

When I woke up the next day, I began to see my daughter from another dimension. She was my daughter, yet she was a personality too. She had a mind of her own, she viewed me as an enemy and treated me like one, and I had to think about my survival. We had to part. I wanted her father to take her for awhile. I needed a break.

I had threatened to send her to her father's several times. I never thought that I really would do it, though. Deep in my gut I've always felt that girls, especially teenage girls, needed to be with the Mother. I went back and forth, sleepless nights wondering about the environment there, the influences in Los Angeles, wondering if we'd ever get back on track again. I was broken, sad and just down right pitiful. My significant other tried to comfort me the best he could and finally we went to the water to pray. I prayed a heart-felt, soul-felt, spirit touching prayer and I felt at peace.

As we were walking across the beach a lady approached us and she spoke and took my hand. "Baby, I know that you are worried about your daughter but, she's gonna be all right. One day she is going to come to you and lie her head on your lap and say I'm sorry." I cried, because I knew that only God could have used her to minister to me.

It was rough on me to let her go. My son was entering college at that same time and I was physically wiped out. She cried and my heart bled for her. I didn't want her to go, yet I felt it was the thing to do to save her life. The negative influences had a hold on her here. She left and I was alone to face my demons and to heal.

I started looking and feeling younger. I didn't even know how much pressure I was under until it was gone. Tons of pressure was removed. It took me months before I realized that I didn't need to be home by 6 or 7, that I was free not to cook, to read all evening, that nobody was going to even call my name. I was in heaven.

Christmas came and my daughter came to visit. She seemed to have changed but I was too afraid to accept it. I kept feeling that it was just a matter of time and she'd show her true colors. She begged to stay and we both knew how weak I was for her. I remained strong and she went back. She finally returned in the spring of the following year and there really had been a change. Changes occurred within her that I could not make occur.

Letting her go was the best thing that could have happened. I missed her and she missed me, yet we had an opportunity to love from afar. There grew a new appreciation for each other. The Creator had been very influential in my daughter's life. Isn't that such a loving thing? I could be with her yet I was afforded an opportunity to know these other women on a certain level of course and to get their insight on her adjustment, struggles, accomplishments etc. We reunited and we are both the better for it.

The author of the following piece is unknown. A friend sent it to me while I was growing through this experience.

LET GO

To "let go" does not mean to stop caring, it means I can't do it for someone else. To "let go" is not to cut myself off, it's the realization I can't control another. To "let go" is to admit powerlessness, which means the outcome is not in my hands. To "let go" is not to try to change or blame another, it's to make the most of myself. To "let go" is not to care for, but to care about. To "let go" is not to fix, but to be supportive. To "let go" is not to be in the middle arranging all the outcomes but to allow others to affect their destinies. To "let go" is not to be protective, it's to permit another to face reality. To "let go" is not to deny, but to accept. To "let go" is not to nag, scold or argue, but instead to search out my own shortcomings and correct them. To "let go" is not to adjust everything to my desires but to take each day as it comes, and cherish myself in it. To "let go" is not to regret the past, but to grow and live for the future. To "let go" is to fear less, and love more.

Parting Thought

I believe that the Mother is THE key player in the home. We are the center. We have the wombs which conceive and re-create. Spirit moved upon the womb of a woman and she gave forth a "son" which would allow us all to become sons and daughters of God.

And now I have risen from the dead and am looking at the kingdom life in every aspect of my life. I am in love with a wonderful man. We had seen each other several times at meetings of a "spiritual" nature. I never knew his name. I had always felt his "goodness" and his "warmth." The friend that was used as a "channel" to bring us together made his transition and Bobbie was part of the "homegoing ceremony." I was sitting with a man whom I had dated for two years. We both knew that it was just a matter of time before we move on our paths. We just didn't know it would be so fast!

Something inside me knew that I had to get to know him on another level. I had a dream about him. In this dream he was in a place where you had to step down in order to enter. I was afraid, Bobbie opened the door, his smile was beautiful and he held his hand out to me. I hesitated and his look said, "You can trust me!" I gave him my hand and saw two other people in this dream, whom I would meet later in the relationship. The man I later found out was one of his best friends and the woman, his "spiritual" mother. Another interesting aspect was that Bobbie had a "diamond" on his forehead. I later found out that he was a licensed gemologist. I loved him from day one and knew that we'd be together. He has opened many doors for me spiritually and has held my hand through the darkest nights. We have our challenges and every one has caused us to grow. We are spiritual partners.

Spiritual partners recognize the existence of the soul, and consciously seek to further its evolution. Loving at the soul level is loving very unselfishly. There are times that Bobbie does things that I dislike. If I am not directly involved in it, it is none of my business. So many times as women we want to raise men, change them, make them better instead of allowing the God within them to teach, guide, reveal, and change them. This in reality is the only way the change comes about anyway.

I have learned to love unconditionally with Bobbie. Sometimes he must be about his Father's business, helping others, and it is in total opposition to what I want him to do with me, for me or for us. I must stop, surrender and ask my Lord, "let thy will be done in this situation, Lord. He has his own soul growth to complete.

We came on this planet to do more than be someone's wife, husband, employee, sibling, parent or child. Those roles are slices of the pie and the whole pie is the growth of the soul.